HE AND SHE
MEN IN THE EIGHTIES

HE AND SHE
MEN IN THE EIGHTIES

YVETTE WALCZAK

ROUTLEDGE
London and New York

First published in 1988 by
Routledge
11 New Fetter Lane, London EC4P 4EE

Published in the USA by
Routledge
in association with Routledge, Chapman & Hall, Inc.
29 West 35th Street, New York NY 10001

© 1988 Yvette Walczak

Printed in Great Britain

All rights reserved. No part of this book may be reprinted or reproduced or utilised in any form or by any electronic, mechanical, or other means, now known or hereafter invented, including photocopying and recording, or in any information storage or retrieval system, without permission in writing from the publishers.

British Library Cataloguing in Publication Data

Walczak, Yvette
 He and she : men in the eighties.
 1. Men   2. Sex role
 I. Title
 305.3'1   HQ1090

ISBN 0-415-00514-0
ISBN 0-415-00515-9 (Pbk)

Library of Congress Cataloging in Publication Data

Walczak, Yvette.
 He and she: men in the eighties/Yvette Walczak.
  p. cm.
 Bibliography: p.
 Includes index.
 ISBN 0-415-00514-0   ISBN 0-415-00515-9 (Pbk)
  1. Men — United States — Attitudes. 2. Men — United States — Interviews. 3. Sex role — United States. I. Title.
 HQ1090.3.W35 1988
 305.3'1'0973 — dc19   87-30418

Printed and bound in Great Britain
by Billing & Sons Limited, Worcester.

Contents

Acknowledgements	vii
Biographical Details	viii
Introduction	1
1. Fifty-one Male Characters	5
2. Women and Men; Yin and Yang	26
3. Similar or Different?	39
4. Education	54
5. Employment	64
6. Relationships	78
7. Housework, Decisions, Finance	98
8. Children	114
9. Changing Attitudes	129
10. Individual Biographies	140
References	159
Index	164

To my daughters, Natalie and Susan,
wishing them well in their choice of men

Acknowledgements

I should like to offer my thanks to friends and colleagues who have given me support, encouragement and advice; only a few of them can be mentioned by name, otherwise the list would be a very long one. I am particularly grateful to all the men who took part in this project. This book could not have been written without their participation. They were all generous with their time and interest.

I have also been helped in a variety of ways by the following: John Hall who offered advice on survey methodology; Sue Joshua of Croom Helm for seeing this book through its final stages; Vivien Onslow who put me in touch with some of the men in this book; Dave Phillips, who commented on the original draft of the questionnaire; Julia Richardson, who helped to arrange the interviews; Naomi Roth, formerly of Croom Helm, without whose encouragement our original idea would never have been translated into a book; and many others.

The project was financed by the Polytechnic of North London.

Biographical Details

Yvette Walczak was born in Poland and has lived, studied and worked in England since 1946. Having read Sociology and Anthropology at the London School of Economics she trained in social work at the Institute of Medical Social Work and the Tavistock Clinic. She teaches on a Social Work Course at the Polytechnic of North London and practises as a family therapist and divorce conciliator. She writes, lectures and broadcasts on marriage and divorce. Her previous book, written with Sheila Burns, *Divorce: the child's point of view*, was published by Harper and Row in 1984. She has two daughters.

Introduction

The population of the United Kingdom according to Census figures recorded on the night of 5/6 April 1981,[86] is made up of almost equal numbers of men (27,050,000) and women (28,626,000). More male than female babies are conceived and born, more females survive – which accounts for the reverse ratio in the older age groups. Does biology determine destiny and are men and women so very different in every respect: intellectually, emotionally and in terms of their social relationships and careers? Alternatively, are they similar creatures falsely presumed to be ideally biologically equipped for a variety of non-interchangeable sex-linked roles?

Much has been written lately about these issues from the basis of female experience in what is often referred to as a 'man's world'. Questions about gender equality, as well as similarities and differences between the sexes, have been addressed both from factual and phenomenological perspectives. The facts about sexism in the fields of education, employment and domestic division of labour have been documented and the experience of being a female employee, a mother and a wife vividly described by women. The aim of this book, and the research on which it is based, has been to explore, analyse and report the male point of view: how men perceive the sexes in relation to each other and how attitudes and normative ideas are translated into everyday behaviour towards female colleagues, girlfriends, wives and other women. For this purpose a number of men were approached and agreed to share with me their views and ideas. These men come from a variety of social and cultural backgrounds, follow a variety of occupations and have been involved in a range of relationships, such as marriage, 'going out' and having a male partner. Some have been through the traumas of divorce or bereavement.

As had been expected, I encountered a wide range of attitudes and modes of behaviour, and often wide discrepancies between professed ideal standards and their implementation in practice – as has been found by a recent major national survey 'British Social Attitudes'.[54] The discrepancy between norms and what people do is not surprising at a time when traditional attitudes towards male/female roles have encountered a strong challenge from more egalitarian aspirations, particularly by women, as well as new

Introduction

explanations for what were once thought to be irreducible differences between the sexes. The concept of androgyny is a relatively new one and based on the assumption that either sex can possess in equal measure characteristics which had been traditionally ascribed to one sex only and presumed to be feminine or masculine.

The three men who will now be introduced by their fictitious names – as will be all the other characters in the book – represent some of the diversities between those who took part in the survey, as well as some similarities. I was reminded of the greater longevity of women during my search for octogenarians. An officer in charge of a residential home for elderly people introduced me to Charlie, aged 90, one of the three male residents among 23 ladies. Charlie has vivid memories of a world which he considers to have been totally different from our contemporary society, with which he keeps in touch through reading a daily newspaper. He has designated working mothers as the cause of juvenile delinquency and the increased incidence of muggings. My question as to whether his wife, Mary, continued to work after they were married was politely interpreted as an aspersion on his ability to have been an adequate provider: 'it was my place to provide . . . Mary gave up her dressmaking career to look after me . . . she was a lovely cook'. Charlie did not altogether opt out of domestic chores, his contribution being washing up the dishes after the evening meal. There was, according to Charlie, 'men's work' and 'women's work'. In spite of changing attitudes, such strict division of domestic labour has remained a major characteristic of British households.[55]

In contrast, before settling down to talk to me, Ranjeev put away his ironing board and explained that although he was brought up in a traditional Indian family, he and his living-in girlfriend share everything, and intend to continue doing this after they have been married. Ranjeev, a nurse in his 20s, has strong egalitarian views and regrets that the pay structure and his greater earning potential may influence their decision about which parent stays at home to look after the children, when these arrive on the scene. Ranjeev confessed to feeling intimidated by some of his more outspoken feminist colleagues, while being able to appreciate that their remarks were not personal, but directed at men generally.

Jeremy, a sculptor in his 60s, described an 'unforgettable experience' which filled him with some degree of envy and admiration. While he watched his neighbour breastfeeding her baby he realised that he, as a man, has never been so close to a child, and he wished that he could have been. Like many men, Jeremy feels that there is a very special bond between a mother and her baby, a closeness which men are deprived of experiencing, enjoying and understanding. He sees some differences and many similarities between men and women.

For many centuries, and in all known societies, there has been a division of labour between males and females, not necessarily resulting in unequal status. The best-known case of role reversal were the Tchambuli of New Guinea, whose customs became known through the writing of the well-known anthropologist, Margaret Mead[72]. The tribe was almost extinct at the time of her visits. She observed women both looking after children and doing heavy work, while men, adorned with paint, gossiped with each other and tackled the less heavy tasks. More traditionally, the outside world has been the domain of men, regardless of whether that world was the jungle and a hunting ground for wild animals, a Welsh coalmine or a Merchant Bank in the City of London. Gathering berries in the forest, and preparation of food under primitive conditions, has been as much 'women's work' as cooking the family meal in a kitchen equipped with every 'appliance of science' ranging from a deep freezer to a microwave oven. While recently listening to a radio programme I heard a man tell the interviewer that he had brought his wife a present from his Italian business trip: a pasta machine. Asked if it worked, he professed ignorance, but promised to enquire from his spouse when he got home that evening.

In many spheres men and women have been assumed to be different; often on the assumption that biological make-up plays a major part in shaping emotions and behaviour from an early age. Such assumed differences can lead to discrimination on the basis of sex. It has also been said by Kate Millett[73] that discrimination calls for psychological theories which justify inequality.

In the past 20 years traditional beliefs have been questioned, and the influence of the Women's Movement, demand for female labour and unemployment among men cannot be overemphasised. A few men have begun to feel and say that in certain ways they are also discriminated against, but not a great deal is known about the experience of being a man in the 1980s. The interest in the male point of view on equality is growing, and is being explored through individual contacts between men, between men and women, through men's groups and such programmes as 'About Men', first shown on Channel 4 Television in September 1983. A well-known psychologist, Rudolph Schaffer, alongside others exploring new ideas about parenting, wrote in his book *Mothering*,[98] 'all the original reasons for confining childcare to women are disappearing: mother need not be a woman'. Some men would like to spend more time with their children; some resent having been socialised as children into believing that 'boy's don't cry'.

Our society embodies many beliefs, standards and ways of behaving, and we are at a crossroads between tradition and innovation. The majority of the population are in favour of the egalitarian principles embodied in the anti-sexist legislation of the 1970s: the Equal Pay Act 1970, and the Sex Discrimination Act 1975,[54] while at the same time the average weekly pay of a woman is just over half that of a man. Irrespective of paid work, women are mostly responsible for household chores. Social policy is often discriminatory, as exemplified by the case of Mrs Drake, a married woman who was refused an invalid care allowance on the grounds of being married and regarded as dependent on a male. The European Court considered this to be a breach of EEC law on sex equality.[53]

Both sexes have a great deal to gain from a more egalitarian approach. Perhaps the way in which men can profit is less tangible than in the case of women. It is my hope that a book such as this may, in small measure, promote better understanding of the sexes, from a more equal footing. I have tried, if not totally succeeded, to ask questions and to write without bias; the search for total objectivity has been described as 'philosophically naive'.[69]

1
Fifty-one Male Characters

Unlike Pirandello's six characters, mine had not searched for an author, the process having been reversed. The *dramatis personae* are introduced below, in alphabetical order rather than in the order of their appearance in the book. All names are fictitious, some having been chosen by the bearer, others by myself, taking into account such factors as the country of birth. No doubt my own fantasies have played some part, reflecting previous encounters with similar persons in real life, the media and literature. It may hardly be a coincidence that the first name on the list is Adam, a symbol of preandrogynous thinking but, strangely, the only male so far able to give birth, albeit from his rib.

> Adam; aged 21; unemployed since leaving school; single; born in England.
> Alex; aged 54; a scientist; divorced; born in England.
> Alf; aged 89; retired commercial traveller; widowed; born in England.
> Barry; aged 20; unemployed unskilled labourer; single; born in England.
> Benjamin; aged 43; clerk; divorced; born in Ghana.
> Bert; aged 87; retired fireman; widowed; born in Scotland.
> Bob; aged 65; probation officer; single; born in England.
> Charlie; aged 90; retired maintenance engineer; widowed twice; born in England.
> Chris; aged 29; merchant banker; single; had cohabited with a woman for seven years; born in England.
> Clifford; aged 64; clerk; single; born in England.
> Costas; aged about 40; social worker; married; born in Cyprus.

Fifty-one Male Characters

Craig; aged 17; manual worker in the catering trade; single; born in England.
Daniel; aged 37; clergyman; married; born in England.
Darren; aged 21; building labourer; married; born in England.
Dennis; aged 45; house painter; married; born in England.
Dick; aged 19; unemployed unskilled labourer; single; born in Wales.
Donald; aged 74; actor; divorced; born in England.
Eamonn; aged 59, social worker; had been married and divorced; cohabited for several years with a women who died recently; born in Ireland.
Frank; aged 50, self-employed builder; married; born in England.
Gerald; aged 36; social worker; born in England.
Graham; aged 45; headmaster; married; born in England.
Harold; aged 55; lecturer; separated; born in Germany.
Hugh; aged 37; university lecturer; single; cohabited for several years with a woman; born in England.
Ivor; aged 65; retired civil service clerk; divorced; born in England.
Jacob; aged 78; retired butcher; widowed; born in England.
Jeremy; aged 62; sculptor; divorced; born in England.
Jimmy; aged 28; unemployed unskilled labourer; single; born in England.
John; aged 36; photographer; married; born in England.
Jonathan; aged 17; unemployed unskilled labourer; single; born in England.
Karmi; aged 48; lecturer; divorced; born in Iraq.
Keith; aged 31; merchant banker; single; born in England.
Kevin; aged 26; unemployed unskilled labourer; single; born in England.
Leroy; aged 23; unemployed panel beater; single; born in Jamaica.
Lionel; aged 55; draughtsman; single; born in England.
Mike; aged 29; building labourer; married; born in England.
Murray; aged 23; student; cohabiting with a woman; born in England.
Nigel; aged early 30s; commercial artist, single; cohabited with a woman; born in England.
Ralph; aged late 50s; teacher; divorced; born in England.

Fifty-one Male Characters

Ramah; aged 19; unemployed since leaving school; single; born in Pakistan.
Ranjeev; aged 26; health visitor; cohabiting with his fiancée; born in Pakistan.
Richard; aged 19; unemployed since leaving school; single; born in England.
Roland; aged 54; personnel officer; divorced; born in England.
Sanjay; aged 32; taxi driver; married; born in India.
Simon; aged 26; labourer; single; born in England.
Stanley; aged 23; money dealer; single; born in England.
Sydney; aged 52; book-keeper; divorced; born in England.
Tom; aged 78; painter/decorator; married; born in England.
Trevor; aged 60; retired bank manager; married; born in England.
Troy; aged 58; retired scientist; divorced; born in England.
Vince; aged 30; nurse; cohabiting with a male partner; born in England.
Vipul; aged 50; care assistant in a home for elderly people; married for the second time (first marriage having ended in divorce); born in Guyana.

In addition to those who are listed above as having fully participated, a number of men who knew about the on-going research have spontaneously contributed their views on matters which were of special interest and concern to them. Among them were my students, colleagues, and friends. One man – a window fitter – who happened to be fitting a new window in my house, upon hearing about the subject of this book handed me his tool box and made a brief but eloquent gesture towards the empty frame, accompanied by words of encouragement; 'here you are, love, get on with it'. Neither of us had any doubts about my ability to install double-glazed windows; possibly, our reasons might have been different. Jack's were based on my gender, mine on the knowledge that many years ago I chose to study sociology rather than to learn how to replace windows and handle power tools. This was the shortest interview, and for this reason Jack has not been included among those listed, apart from this brief mention.

It had been my aim to gather information from about 50 men, who would represent a wide age range, a variety of occupations – including those who have retired and a few who have been unemployed for various lengths of time. Among the youngest men, I expected to include those who had been unable to find work since leaving school. Because of the variety of occupations, all social classes were to be spanned in terms of the Registrar General's classification. Among those men some would be single, others married, a number divorced and a few widowed. The sample was to include men who were currently cohabiting or had cohabited with women or men. Overall, they would have been involved in a whole range of intimate relationships, both heterosexual and homosexual. Some of the men would have children or even grandchildren. As we live in a multiracial society I had intended to make contact with men from different ethnic backgrounds, those born in this country and those born elsewhere. With regards to early background and education, my aim was again a heterogeneous rather than a homogeneous group: some from 'working-class' and others from 'middle-class' families of origin.

The youngest man, in the event, was 17 years old and the eldest had celebrated his 90th birthday a few days prior to our meeting. The great majority of men were quite willing to tell me their exact age – unnecessarily, I had anticipated some reticence over this, and gave them the choice of indicating a broad category (Table 1.1).

Table 1.1: Age at interview

17–19	5
20–29	12
30–39	9
40–49	5
50–59	9
60–69	5
70–79	4
80 and over	2
Total	51

The 73 years which separate 17-year-old Craig and Charlie, aged 90, (still in good health and enjoying his lifelong hobby of painting his own landscapes as well as copying famous paintings), have seen some major upheavals and many significant changes. Many things have not changed. There have been two major wars. Among the demographic changes, the overall birth rates have fallen, though subject to fluctuations such as the baby boom of the 1950s. Both men and women marry younger, though there has been a recent reversal of the trend. Everyone has a chance to live longer, while old age has come to be seen by some people as a social problem. While there has been a change in expressed beliefs, in many spheres behaviour remains the same and, in spite of such book titles as *Goodbye Father*[44] and *Goodbye Tarzan*[34], we have not bid farewell to men like Mike, who says 'I don't know one end of the hoover from the other', who relies on his bread-winning capacity to sustain his wife's love, and does not seem to feel uneasy about spending very little time with his children, who are usually ready for bed by the time he gets home in the evening after a day's work on a building site.

There have been many changes in the employment situation for men and women, but the old fears and prejudices remain, and while the trade unions may support equal pay, often the reasons are based on fear of competition and a lower rate for all rather than the ideal of equality. In wartime, while men were away in the forces, women had to fill in the gap and enter occupations considered to be a male domain, including the engineering trade and ammunition factories. According to Elizabeth Wilson,[109] before 1914 many women were already in paid employment – as many as five and a half million – mostly in female occupations such as textile work, clerical jobs, teaching and nursing. During the 1914–18 war the number of women in paid employment increased by nearly two million, but the corresponding increase (discounting the overall trend) for the 1939–43 period was less than a million. To some extent the war brought greater equality between the sexes, of a somewhat temporary nature. Once the heroes returned home, most of the women withdrew to make room for them. It was in the 1950s that married women, specially middle-class ones, entered the labour market in significant numbers.

Poverty has always been a feature of our society, and has been shown to exist even today.[105] At the same time, the trend has been towards a higher standard of living, particularly in the 1950s and 1960s, with the working classes always behind the middle classes, and in terms of affluence and aspirations, the classes separated by a distance of several years. This phenomenon has been referred to as a 'marching column',[113] the tail of which is always behind its head, but with the whole procession always moving on. This trend and difference has affected the way people spend their leisure time and allocate spending priorities. More people own cars, television sets and labour-saving devices, while the average woman still spends almost as much time in the kitchen, compared with her husband, as she did 70 years ago.

Educational opportunities have improved both for men and women. More young people stay on at school beyond the statutory school-leaving age, which in 1972 was raised from 15 to 16. At the same time, a career in science, engineering and the old-established professions such as law and medicine remains predominantly a male prerogative. Only a man can serve God as a Roman Catholic priest. Some careers have partly lost their 'men-only' label. In the late 1940s permanent civil service and teaching posts became open to married women, until then banned from applying.

In the sphere of personal relationships, 'marriage has never been more popular if it has never been more risky'.[50] With some fluctuations and recent trend reversal there has been an overall tendency towards younger marriages, while the institution has remained as popular as ever. Around 90 per cent of the adult population gets married. In 1982 the median age at marriage was 23.5 for women and 25.9 for men.[21] What has changed significantly is the set of expectations which men and women profess to bring into marriage, and the proportion of couples who remain married to each other for life. According to two nationwide surveys carried out by a British anthropologist, Geoffrey Gorer, in 1950[42] and 1969[43], at the earlier date great admiration was attached to the conventional male virtue of being a good provider, and female excellence at domestic and mothering skills. Nearly 20 years later, good communication and companionship were top of the list.

Divorce rates were fairly consistent at the beginning of the century. There was a sharp increase at the end of 1918, the peak year for that period being 1919. After 1921 there was a levelling off and another sharp increase from 1941 onwards, particularly between 1945 and 1947, after which the rate decreased. According to Fletcher,[33] a sociologist, 'war disturbs human relationships at the most intimate level'. In my view such a change is often desirable. Absence, in many cases, does not make the heart grow fonder but imposes an added strain; it is also possible that increased economic independence of women in wartime, and different expectations, have been the cause of most divorces. In 1950, legal aid became generally available for divorce, and this coincided with another sharp increase. In 1984 there were 154,000 divorces in the United Kingdom, the rate having doubled since the Divorce Reform Act 1969 became law in 1971.

Some two-thirds of divorced people remarry; in 1985 there were 175,000 divorces. One third of all marriages were a remarriage for one or both partners.[21]

Views on sexual morality have also changed. Official cohabitation figures are likely to be underestimates, since many people do not like to admit that they are living together, for fear of losing some social security benefits. It has been estimated that 10 per cent of young women aged 20-29 cohabit without being married. Premarital sex is acceptable to almost half the population – especially young people – while extramarital relationships are considered by 58 per cent to be always wrong, and considered mostly wrong by 25 per cent of those who took part in the British Social Attitudes Survey, 1984.[54] Sexual activity has been largely separated from procreation. There has been a steady trend to smaller families, and sex has come to be seen as enjoyable in its own right.

The number of single-parent households has increased. There are no official statistics prior to 1967. In 1950 there were some 500,000 as compared with almost one million currently.[77] Such families have always existed, due to bereavement or absence of men during the war, but have more recently been defined as a social problem in many publications. Some 95,000 fathers head one-parent households, and the legitimacy of this role was recognised when single fathers became entitled in 1979 to social security benefits on par with single mothers, without the condition of having to be available for work.

The quest for equality found reflection in legislation in the shape of the Equal Pay Act 1970, and the Guardianship Act 1973, which gave mothers and fathers equal rights as custodians of their children; until then the father had been considered the child's legal guardian. The Sex Discrimination Act 1975 was another egalitarian measure and, more doubtfully, the Matrimonial Proceedings Act 1984, designed to implement the principle of a 'clear break' on divorce.

The structure of social security benefits continues to reflect the assumption that a man is responsible for supporting his woman and children. This assumption was incorporated into the National Assistance Act, 1948, and twenty-five years later into the Social Security Act 1973. This, in a few instances, militates against men also. 'Why cannot I claim a widower's pension?' complained one of my informants with bitterness in his voice.

The men who took part in the study are in a variety of working situations. A person's occupation determines his income, lifestyle and range of potential choices. An affluent couple may not need to choose which parent stays at home to look after the children, since employing a nanny is within their reach. 'If we did not want to cook we could eat out', said one of the better-off informants. The men include unskilled, semi-skilled and skilled manual workers such as building labourers, cleaners, roofers, a fireman, a butcher, a maintenance engineer and a taxi driver. White-collar workers comprise clerks, administrators, a book-keeper and a commercial traveller. Among the professional men are scientists, a priest, bankers, a money dealer, teachers, an actor, a sculptor, nurses, social workers and a personnel officer. Ten men are currently unemployed, of whom four have been unable to find work since leaving school. All the unemployed have no particular skills, and those who have worked have had a variety of short-lasting jobs. Four of these young men are on the government-sponsored Community Enterprise Programme created for people out of work (those aged 18–24 who had been out of work for at least six months out of nine, and those aged over 25 who had been out of work for 12 months. Those who are on the project are mostly doing excavation work. The unemployed seem to have a feeling of hopelessness about their career prospects and a few professed to prefer this way of life to the 'rat race', giving preference to being able to travel to Stonehenge and playing loud music over being harnessed to a boring manual job. While there is little chance of finding work, they have a lifestyle alternative to being gainfully employed. One of the men is a full-time student who had not worked, and the other two full-time students are qualified nurses. Seven men have been retired for varying lengths of time, two of them before the age of 65. Table 1.2 sets out occupational status.

Table 1.2: Occupational status

Employed	31
Retired	7
Unemployed (who have previously worked)	6
Unemployed (since leaving school)	4
Students	3
Total	51

The Registrar General's classification into social classes is based on occupation, and on this basis the men were spread among all the classes (using the OPCS classification).[85] (See Table 1.3)

Table 1.3: Social class

I	(Professional and managerial)	6
II	(Intermediate)	16
IIInm	(Skilled non-manual occupations)	7
IIIm	(Skilled manual occupations)	6
IV	(Partly skilled)	5
V	(Unskilled)	6
	Students	1
	Unemployed since leaving school	4
	Total	51

Note: Students, unemployed and retired men who had previously been employed are allocated on the basis of their last occupation.

The men are currently, and have been in the past, involved in a variety of intimate relationships (Table 1.4), representing the diversity of the modern family and living styles. Apart from 13 of the 17 single men, all the others have had long-lasting relationships with women. One is living with a male partner. Four single men had had long-lasting relationships in the past, which ended for a variety of reasons which will be discussed in Chapter 5 on personal relationships. Two of these ended when the partner died. Of the three men currently cohabiting, one is living with a male partner. Fourteen men have been divorced and have not remarried. Of the four widowers, one had been married and widowed twice.

Table 1.4: Intimate relationships

Single	19
Cohabiting	3
Married	13
Divorced/Separated	12
Widowed	4
Total	51

Table 1.5: Ethnic origins

Cyprus	1
England	40
Ghana	1
Guyana	1
India	1
Iraq	1
Ireland	1
Pakistan	2
Scotland	1
Wales	1
West Indies	1
Total	51

Ours is a society in which different races and cultures are well represented: 6 per cent of the population are immigrants from other countries.[20] The largest ethnic minority are Indian in origin (see Table 1.5), the second largest West Indian, followed by Guyanese and Pakistani groups. There are also people born in European countries, the Middle East and the Far East. All those interviewed born outside England have settled here, and do not intend to return to their countries of origin, with the exception of a young man born in Pakistan. He has visited his relatives who still live there and has no intention of going through the trauma of an English marriage. He expects his parents, aided by relatives, to help arrange his marriage and looks forward to traditional marital contentment. He intends to return to Pakistan in his mid-20s when the time comes for him to 'marry and settle down'. Those men who have made their home here remember well their traditional backgrounds, and provide interesting insights into cultural differences which will be referred to throughout the book. At the time of the interview all the men were living or working in the Greater London area.

When asked about their families of origin, what work their parents did and whether they would describe them as 'working-class' or 'middle-class' the majority said they came from working-class backgrounds (Table 1.6).

Asked about education, almost half the men indicated that they left school at the earliest opportunity (Table 1.7). One of these described himself as mentally handicapped, and he had to have 'special education'. Twenty-seven men had some form of education beyond school-leaving age, including staying on at school,

Table 1.6: Family of origin

Working-class	31
Middle-class	20
Total	51

Table 1.7: Education

Left school at school-leaving age	24
Further education (other than a degree)	16
Higher education (to at least first degree level)	11
Total	51

evening classes and short vocational courses; eleven men went to a university or a polytechnic and read a variety of subjects.

Some of the men appear to have reached well-paid and responsible positions without having had much formal further education. All the unemployed were either semi-skilled or unskilled and had had no training after leaving school – apart from those on the Community Enterprise Programme.

Almost all of the contacts with the people interviewed were made in the same way. Originally they all received a standard letter explaining that I was researching men's views and ideas about gender equality and on differences and similarities between the sexes. Those willing to take part were invited to get in touch with me and feel free to ask for further information. In a few cases the original contact was made by another person, when it was thought that such an introduction would be useful as a guarantee of confidentiality and secure cooperation. In the case of four elderly men resident in homes for old people, the initial approach was made to the officers in charge, who acted as intermediaries.

In the old people's homes men are a tiny minority, and in each of the four homes only one male resident was able to take part, but those who did enjoyed the opportunity not only of expressing their views, but generally talking about the past, their life histories, entertaining me with jokes and fascinating accounts of past events, as well as showing me old photographs, letters and personal belongings.

Most of the young men written to were at the time living in a hostel for homeless young people, and some were their friends, living in a squat. They all agreed to take part with a high degree of willingness and helpfulness. Most of the divorced men are members of a social club for divorced and separated people. They have been divorced for various lengths of time and have not remarried. Divorced and single status is a condition of membership of that particular club. A member of the club's committee kindly agreed to circulate my letter to members living in London. Those few who did not wish to be interviewed explained that they had nothing or very little to say on the subject.

A number of men approached are members of staff of an educational establishment, and all those approached expressed willingness to take part, with one exception who gave a similar reason to that given by the divorced men: he did not think he had any views worth contributing. Thirty students of the same establishment were written to via their pigeonholes, but the response rate was amazingly low, resulting in only three interviews.

A small geographical area in East London was selected and, again, everyone approached consented to the interview. A self-employed builder and the men working for him at the time were also asked, and agreed to take part in this study. The overall response rate was high, and the extremely low rate among the students approached will remain a mystery. A sample collected in this way is, of course, not random, and no claim is made to it being representative.

The interviews took place in a variety of settings which paralleled the diversity of the group interviewed and different lifestyles of the men involved. The settings themselves were often a fit background for the issues being discussed. When I visited the homes for the elderly – one of them run by a religious organisation, the other three owned privately – I was welcomed by either the officer in charge or another staff member, in each case a female. In one instance, while sitting in the hall and waiting to be introduced to the elderly gentleman, I observed a uniformed female nurse trying to reassure a highly agitated old lady. These men, who during the interviews kept referring to having been 'looked after by their wives', were now also being cared for mainly by females. There are, of course, also male carers in such homes, but they constitute a tiny minority – as I was reminded by one of the interviewees, who is himself a care assistant and firmly believes that females are 'kinder and gentler'. This was his own assessment, but he impressed me as a kind and gentle person himself. Most of the youngest unemployed men were seen at the hostel where they currently live. The ethos there is an egalitarian one, and both the young men and women are expected to do their share of cooking and household chores. In fact, most of the cooking is done by a young man, who happens to like doing it and who very kindly invited me to supper with some of his fellow residents. Other young men were seen at their temporary lodgings, a few of them having discarded their middle-class backgrounds for a more colourful itinerant lifestyle. One of them lives with his mother for part of the year, and shares his room with several friends with whom he travels to various pop festivals in a van which he himself had repaired and refurbished, and the interior of which he showed me with some pride and pleasure.

On the same day as I was offered hospitality at a vicarage, where I talked with the incumbent who lives there with his family, I found myself in the vicinity of the Bank of England and the Stock Exchange, a totally male domain until the last world war, and where women are still in a minority. Inside the financial establishment, where I was expected, I was conducted by a uniformed attendant to a meeting room where international financial deals are discussed, and I imagined that there are very few women on the Board of Directors. I was later told by the man, who is responsible for making some of the most important decisions concerning high finance, that not only are women members far outnumbered by male members, the women also need to be very good, and some are better than many men. I was told that if a woman is good-looking as well as good at her job, the chance of her getting a secretarial job are much higher than those of a 'plain-looking girl' with the same ability and qualifications. His own secretary was described as someone who was excellent at her job, efficient and really nice to look at, this being considered an ideal combination.

My choice of method of gathering information was partly determined by the aims of the research, and partly my own background. Since the object was to obtain very detailed information, in-depth interviews seemed best suited to this purpose. The interviews were semi-structured, and this gave me the opportunity to ask about what I was interested in, and allowed the men themselves to contribute information which they considered relevant. My professional experience as a family therapist and divorce conciliator has involved me in interviews which are partly structured by myself and my colleagues, but the content is provided by those taking part, and they hopefully feel free to tell me whatever they want to. The questions included in the questionnaire fall into four main categories: those asking for factual information such as age and occupation; questions about perceived similarities, differences and equality; questions about attitude formation and change; and questions about actual behaviour.

My early anthropological training and encounters with anthropologists who had done field work made me acutely aware of discrepancies between professed beliefs and how these are and are not implemented into the minutiae of everyday living and behaviour. Anthropologists preceded sociologists in noticing and drawing attention to these differences. While stranded in the Trobriand Islands during the first World War, Bronislaw Malinowski[68] discovered that because of the strong brother/sister taboo a man who perchance comes across his sister making love to a man is supposed to commit suicide by jumping down from a high palm tree. A little later he found that such men preferred to look the other way. Recent surveys of British social attitudes (already mentioned)[54,55] confirm the discrepancy between normative beliefs and behaviour in relation to housework and looking after children.

The questionnaire reproduced below served as *aide-memoire*, full comments being invited on each item, rather than a 'yes' or 'no' answer.

QUESTIONNAIRE (used as an *aide-memoire*)

1. *Age*
    - (a) 17-19
    - (b) 20-29
    - (c) 30-39
    - (d) 40-49
    - (e) 50-59
    - (f) 60-69
    - (g) 70-79
    - (h) 80 and over

    (Either exact age or category to be given)

2. *Occupation*
    - (a) Employed
    - (b) Unemployed
    - (c) Retired
    - (d) Student

3. *Social class* (Registrar General classification)
   (a) I
   (b) II
   (c) III non-manual
   (d) III manual
   (e) IV
   (f) V
4. *Country of origin*
5. *Marital status*
   (a) Single
   (b) Married (number of times)
   (c) Cohabiting
   (d) Divorced
   (e) Other relationships
   (f) Widowed
6. *Family of origin*
   (a) Father's occupation (main)
   (b) Mother's occupation (main)
   (c) General family background (e.g. how parents divided their roles)
7. *Education*
   (a) State
   (b) Private
   (c) Higher
   (d) Further
8. *Age completed*
   (a) Earliest school-leaving age
   (b) Beyond school-leaving age

Similarities and differences

9. Are men and women the same, and if 'no' what are the main differences?

   Intellectually
   (a) Yes
   (b) No
   Comments and reasons
   Emotionally
   (c) Yes

(d) No
Comments and reasons
Interests
(e) Yes
(f) No
Comments and reasons
Aptitudes
(g) Yes
(h) No
Comments and reasons
Social relationships, e.g. friendships
(i) Yes
(j) No
Comments and reasons
Intimate relationships (e.g. expectations and behaviour)
(k) Yes
(l) No
Comments and reasons

Education

10. Should boys and girls have the same type of education (e.g. content, type)?
    (a) Yes
    (b) No
    Comments and reasons

Employment

11. Are men and women capable of doing the same type of work?
    (a) Yes
    (b) No
    Comments and reasons

12. Should men and women get equal pay for the same type of work?
    (a) Yes
    (b) No
    Comments and reasons

Couple relationships

13. Should men and women feel equally free to initiate a relationship?
    (a) Yes
    (b) No
    Comments and reasons

14. On occasions when a couple go out together, who should pay (e.g. for meals, tickets, etc.)?
    (a) Man
    (b) Woman
    (c) Equal shares
    Comments and reasons

Sexual relationships

15. Should both partners behave in a similar way (e.g. initiate sex, be monogamous)?
    (a) Yes
    (b) No
    Comments and reasons

Marriage/stable cohabitation

16. Who should make major decisions (e.g. about contraception, buying property, where to reside, work, holidays)?
    (a) Man
    (b) Woman
    (c) Jointly
    (d) According to type of decision
    Comments and reasons

Finance

17. If both partners are working, what is a fair arrangement?
    (a) All money be pooled
    (b) Some money to be pooled to pay for joint expenses
    (c) Man have responsibility for household expenses

(d) Woman have responsibility for household expenses (House expenses = rent, mortgages, bills, food, etc.)
(e) Other arrangements
Comments and reasons

18. If only the man is working, should his income be considered as joint?
(a) Yes
(b) No
Comments and reasons

19. If only the woman is working, should her income be considered as joint?
(a) Yes
(b) No
Comments and reasons

Housework/maintenance

20. If both partners are working should they be equally responsible for the following tasks?
Shopping
(a) Yes
(b) No
Cooking
(c) Yes
(d) No
Washing up
(e) Yes
(f) No
Laundry
(g) Yes
(h) No
Cleaning
(i) Yes
(j) No
Gardening
(k) Yes
(l) No
Car repairs
(m) Yes
(n) No

Household repairs/Maintenance (e.g. electrical appliances)
(o) Yes
(p) No
Entertaining (e.g. friends and relatives)
(q) Yes
(r) No
Comments and reasons

Child rearing

21. If both partners wish to work, but do not want their baby looked after by anyone other than themselves, who should stay at home and give up work?
    (a) Mother
    (b) Father
    Comments and reasons

22. Who is the best person to care for a baby under 1 year old?
    (a) Mother
    (b) Father
    (c) Both equally
    (d) Each better at certain tasks
    Comments and reasons

23. Who is the best person to look after a child 1–4 years old?
    (a) Mother
    (b) Father
    (c) Both equally
    (d) Each better at certain tasks
    Comments and reasons

24. Who is the best person to look after school-aged children?
    (a) Mother
    (b) Father
    (c) Both equally
    (d) Each better at certain tasks
    Comments and reasons

Attitude formation

25. What factors have influenced your views?
    (a) Parents
    (b) Friends
    (c) Media
    (d) Own thinking and experience
    (e) Other
    Comments and reasons

General

26. In your view, have men and women achieved equality in the following fields?

Education	(a)	yes	(b)	no
Employment	(c)	yes	(d)	no
Pay	(e)	yes	(f)	no
Child-rearing	(g)	yes	(h)	no
Marriage	(i)	yes	(j)	no

    Comments and reasons

Personal

27. If you are or have been married, what are/were the arrangements in your household (marriage includes cohabitation)?
    (a) Decision-making
    (b) Employment
    (c) Finance
    (d) Housework
    (e) Childbirth, child-rearing

28. Additional information, not included in above questions.

The interviews, although similar in structure, varied greatly in duration and how much detail was provided. The shorter ones took less than an hour, the longer ones more than two hours. The shorter ones tended to be with the youngest age group, not because of their unwillingness to talk, but more likely because they had not had a great deal of life experience. Those who have been to single-sex schools and have never worked have had fewer dealings with women than older men, who have worked alongside women, perhaps competed and have had close personal relationships with them. This does not mean that older men have given the subject of equality a great deal more thought than the youngest, many of whom seemed to be very aware of, and to have considered, the issues involved. The longest interviews were with those who felt strongly for personal reasons or on a matter of principle. The four eldest men were so delighted to have my undivided attention, in an environment in which they have few outside visitors, that they seemed truly disappointed when we had to part, and did all they could to prolong our meeting. It has been found that, on the whole, when interviewed about personal matters men talk less easily about their feelings and in less detail than women. In this study I found that there were as many men who seemed happy to talk at length about their views and feelings as those who preferred to confine themselves to facts. A good example of those who spoke openly about emotions was Alex, a scientist, whose fiancée died in tragic circumstances as a result of a road accident. He invited me to read some of the poems he wrote after he had lost her, and we were both deeply moved by the depth of his feelings and sorrow.

In accordance with recent tradition I have described quite fully the method employed, and the characteristics of those who took part in this project. All methods of research have their drawbacks as well as advantages. Large-scale surveys have the advantage of gathering data from large, representative samples, but are not well suited to obtaining detailed answers and learning about minutiae of daily living. Postal and self-completed questionnaires have a high non-response rate. Participant observation is both a passive method, and one in which the presence of the observer may well influence the behaviour of those taking part. Those conducting laboratory experiments often falsely assume that they can recreate real-life situations. Asking questions in a face-to-face situation introduces a bias, which at least can be honestly acknowledged. I am a feminist in so far as I believe that socially bestowed gender has been and still is the basis of discrimination and inequality. There will have to be many changes before the balance is redressed. I do not pretend to know the answer to the question whether men and women are in every way the same.

2
Women and Men; Yin and Yang

Adam and Eve and all humankind, according to the Bible, embarked upon their existence in Paradise. We might still be there if it were not for the power struggle between the first man and the first woman. Their relationship was characterised by tensions and contradictions. She was both weaker and stronger: having been created by a male god from Adam's rib, in the end she won the struggle between herself and her partner. Not only were Adam and Eve different physically, their personalities were different and the idea of sex and gender was firmly established at the beginning of human history. Since 'sex' and 'gender' are different concepts they need clarifications:

> 'Sex' refers to biological differences between men and women mainly in terms of differences in procreative function. 'Gender', however, is a cultural concept relating to the social classification of 'masculine' and 'feminine' and it refers to the ways in which these are socially constructed and sustained and can, therefore, be changed.[90]

Humankind has lived through a number of wars between tribes, nations and factions. Two world wars are within living memory of some of the oldest men who are the subject of this book. The relationship between the sexes has been described as *The Longest War*.[103] This relationship has been based on love, admiration and complementarity as well as tensions, distrust, inequality, competition, envy and mystique.

The notion of male/female differences, other than purely biological and reproductive, has been present throughout history, and was deeply embodied in ancient philosophy. It had been

Women and Men; Yin and Yang

cherished for nearly 5000 years before the Chinese philosopher Lao-tzu (604–531 BC) wrote about it in his book *Tao Teh Ching*. It was expanded by Confucius. The male and female elements in nature are referred to as Yin (female) and Yang (male) and thought to be responsible for all the movement and change. The Yang movement thrusts forward and the Yin motion pulls back; the vital energy, Chi, always flowing between them. Originally, Yang meant the light and Yin the dark side of the mountain. Yin and Yang represent the balancing principle of nature, both necessary and complementary, with different characteristics (Table 2.1).

Table 2.1: Yin and Yang

Yin	Yang
negative	positive
passive	active
female	male
receptive	creative
dark	light
night	day
cold	heat
soft	hard
wet	dry
winter	summer
shadow	sun

Source: Wing[110]

The *I Ching*,[51] the Ancient Chinese Book of Wisdom, is based on the same principles of complementary and opposing forces. The origins of the Treatise are attributed to four holy men (not women): Fu Hsi, King Wen, the Duke of Chou and Confucius. It was translated into English by a missionary, James Legge in the nineteenth century. In the martial art of Tai Chi Chu'an, which is practised all over the world, each movement is either Yin or Yang. Both can be equally effective and powerful.

The idea of differentness and complementarity was carried forward in the work and writings of the psychoanalysts Freud and Jung. Freud was on much more familiar ground when describing the psychosexual development of males than of females, whom he considered to be more of an enigma. Although he did acknowledge social influences, he saw female anatomy as the main cause of a woman's lifelong envy of the penis and the male generally. While regarding men and women as different, he also acknowledged that masculinity and femininity are poles on a continuum and each sex possesses some of the characteristics of the opposite sex. Unconscious rather than conscious processes, according to Freud, link gender and biology.[35]

The notion of differentness and complementarity is a strong theme in Jung's theories about psychic structures and development. Jung evolved the concept of persona: an outwardly adopted mask and the soul: the inner, unconscious self. These are, according to him, complementary. An outwardly feminine woman has a masculine soul (animus) and an outwardly masculine man a feminine soul (anima). The more exaggerated the outward characteristics, the more pronounced their counterparts in the inner self and the more strongly denied. Outward hardness is complemented by inner softness, and vice-versa. Female characteristics are described by Jung as weakness and impressionability and male as strength, logic and objectivity.

> A woman's consciousness is characterised more by the connective quality of Eros than by the discrimination and cognition of Logos. In men, Eros, the function of relationship is usually less developed than Logos. In women, on the other hand, Eros is an expression of their true nature, while their Logos is often only a regrettable accident.[102]

Animus, the unconscious maleness in women, and anima, unconscious femaleness in men, in a well-adjusted person are accepted and integrated with the persona. This view seems to embody a contradiction: why should an 'inferior' set of characteristics be integrated within the psyche of a mature person? Also, why are negative values assigned to female characteristics? They could merit positive connotation. 'Timidity' could be relabelled 'caution', and 'bravery' in some circumstances 'foolishness'. Often, labels ignore the context of behaviour.

The notion of a weak, unclean woman and a pure, strong man is reflected in many rituals and religions such as Judaism and Islam. The Koran equates menstruation with pollution. In medieval times it was usually women, rather than men, who were 'found' to be witches and burnt alive. The well-known treatise on witchcraft written in the fifteenth century, *Malleus Maleficarum* (Witches' Hammer), warned against females' susceptibility to consorting with the devil, because of their desire for sex. It was not until the nineteenth century that women came to be regarded as having purer, and men more animal, natures. Women have been thought to be at the mercy of their bodies, as in the case of hysteria, believed to be caused by a detached, wandering womb, until the illness was given more serious consideration by Freud and Brewer.[36]

In the 1970s the American psychologist Inge Broverman researched stereotypes of male and female characteristics and their respective desirability on the basis of ratings on a seven-point scale. Generally, more male than female traits were seen as preferable, and this is shown in Table 2.2.

Table 2.2: 'Masculine' and 'feminine' characteristics seen as undesirable

(a) Masculine pole is more desirable

Feminine	Masculine
Not at all aggressive	Very aggressive
Not at all independent	Very independent
Very emotional	Not at all emotional
Does not hide emotions at all	Almost always hides emotions
Very subjective	Very objective
Very easily influenced	Not at all easily influenced
Very submissive	Very dominant
Dislikes maths and science very much	Likes maths and science very much
Very excitable in a minor crisis	Not at all excitable in a minor crisis
Very passive	Very active
Not at all competitive	Very competitive
Very illogical	Very logical
Very home-oriented	Very worldly
Not at all skilled in business	Very skilled in business
Very sneaky	Very direct
Does not know the way of the world	Knows the way of the world
Feelings easily hurt	Feelings not easily hurt
Not at all adventurous	Very adventurous
Has difficulty making decisions	Can make decisions very easily
Cries very easily	Never cries
Almost never acts as a leader	Almost always act as a leader
Not at all self-confident	Very self-confident
Very uncomfortable about being aggressive	Not at all uncomfortable about being aggressive
Not at all ambitious	Very ambitious
Unable to separate feelings from ideas	Easily able to separate feelings from ideas
Very dependent	Not at all dependent
Very conceited about appearance	Never conceited about appearance
Thinks women are always superior to men	Thinks men are always superior to women
Does not talk freely about sex with men	Talks freely about sex with men

Table 2.2: Continued

(b) Feminine pole is more desirable

Feminine	Masculine
Doesn't use harsh language at all	Uses very harsh language
Very talkative	Not at all talkative
Very tactful	Very blunt
Very aware of feeling of others	Not at all aware of feelings of others
Very religious	Not at all religious
Very interested in own appearance	Not at all interested in own appearance
Very neat in habits	Very sloppy in habits
Very quiet	Very loud
Very strong need for security	Very little need for security
Enjoys art and literature	Does not enjoy art and literature at all
Easily expresses tender feelings	Does not express tender feelings at all easily

Source: Broverman et al.[15]

Not all well-known theoreticians have stressed male superiority. Analysts other than Freud and Jung have described some advantages of being a female, and the envy felt by men. Among those who attributed positive characteristics to women are Melanie Klein, Karen Horney and Bruno Bettelheim. They drew attention to how much men can envy the woman's ability to bear and nourish children. Such customs as couvade, which embody many elaborate rituals at the time of birth, give men something to do, and put their importance on par with the mother.

In the 1970s American psychologist Sandra Bem,[8] on the basis of extensive research, identified a number of characteristics which are thought to be desirable according to the person's sex. There is also a list of 'neutral' attributes, equally 'desirable' in a male or a female. Bem's inventory is reproduced in full in Table 2.3.

While most men and women tend to choose characteristics typed as 'masculine' or 'feminine' when describing themselves, there are also individuals who cross the boundary and see themselves as possessing both sets in equal measure, as well as 'neutral' ones. Bem concludes that highly sex-typed individuals are not necessarily most mentally healthy, because their rigidity limits the range of options available to them in coping with different types of situations.

A number of theoretical explanations have been put forward to

Table 2.3: Items on the masculinity, femininity and social desirability scale

Masculine items	Feminine items	Neutral items
49. Acts as a leader	11. Affectionate	51. Adaptable
46. Aggressive	5. Cheerful	36. Conceited
58. Ambitious	50. Childlike	9. Conscientious
22. Analytical	32. Compassionate	60. Conventional
13. Assertive	53. Does not use harsh language	45. Friendly
10. Athletic		15. Happy
55. Competitive	35. Eager to soothe hurt feelings	3. Helpful
4. Defends own beliefs		48. Inefficient
37. Dominant	20. Feminine	24. Jealous
19. Forceful	14. Flatterable	39. Likeable
25. Has leadership abilities	59. Gentle	6. Moody
	47. Gullible	21. Reliable
7. Independent	56. Loves children	30. Secretive
52. Individualistic	17. Loyal	33. Sincere
31. Makes decisions easily	26. Sensitive to the needs of others	42. Solemn
		57. Tactful
40. Masculine	8. Shy	12. Theatrical
1. Self-reliant	38. Soft-spoken	27. Truthful
34. Self-sufficient	23. Sympathetic	18. Unpredictable
16. Strong personality	44. Tender	54. Unsystematic
43. Willing to take a stand	29. Understanding	
	41. Warm	
48. Willing to take risks	2. Yielding	

The number preceding each item reflects the position of each adjective as it actually appears on the Inventory.
Source: Bem.[8]

account for differences and inequality. Biological determinists argue that hormones, anatomical and physiological differences give rise to a wide range of other differences. Professor Goldberg,[40] author of the *Inevitability of Patriarchy*, defines patriarchy as male occupancy of high-status positions, and argues that superior physical strength is associated with mental advantage, particularly at the level of genius. Strangely enough for a scientist, he believes that stereotypes are accurate because they are based on observations of a large number of people. One could also argue that because a large number of people used to believe that the earth is flat their view should not have been challenged. Evolutionary explanations draw attention to superior male strength being necessary for survival and protection of women, and that females were confined to the vicinity of their home because of their childbearing function. It is sociological insights which seem to offer most fruitful explanations – social distinctions between males and females are embodied in social institutions, and it is the economy which largely dictates the value placed on male and female labour. More specifically, feminist analysis draws attention to sexual inequalities and stereotypes which serve a useful function of maintaining the *status quo* and confining women to the home and less prestigious and less well-paid jobs.

Although this book is about adults, it would not be possible to understand the nature of male/female differences without some reference to childhood. Metaphorically, human life begins with a 'twinkle in the parents' eyes', though the parent more often referred to seems to be 'daddy'. Biologically, conception takes place when 23 pairs of chromosomes combine, each parent contributing one half of the pairs. Only one of these pairs determines the baby's sex, an XX combination resulting in a girl and XY in a boy, the male parent contributing either X or Y, which determines the embryo's sex. It is surprising that on the basis of such a small genetic difference such widely different characteristics go into the making of gender stereotypes (traits attributed, often falsely, on the basis on one single characteristic: sex).

The development of boys and girls prenatally and between birth and puberty follows a similar pattern, and throughout life differences between individuals can be as great and greater than those between the sexes. On the basis of what is known – and this is not everything – male and female embryos look alike until some six weeks after conception, when internal sex organs begin to look different and male ones develop earlier. The testosterone produced in the male testes stimulates the growth of external sex organs. The ovaries of a female embryo do not secrete female hormones.

More males than females are born: 106 to every 100. Boys' perinatal (around birth) mortality rates are higher, and males seem to be more vulnerable. Boys and girls look remarkably alike, apart from their genitals, unless there is some atypical development due to hormonal or other abnormalities. Boys are slightly longer and heavier at birth, and continue to grow faster until seven months when girls start growing quicker until the age of four years. Boys in infancy have been found to be slightly more restless and sleep less. The secretion of male and female hormones between birth and puberty is minimal, and it is only at puberty that the physical and sexual growth and development follow a significantly different pattern for each sex.

'Puberty' derives from the Latin 'pubertas' meaning (significantly) 'age of *mankind*'. Hormonal secretion, and increased hormone level, precede visible changes. Signals originating in the hypothalamus (a coordinating brain centre) trigger off a chain reaction, via the pituitary gland and other endocrine glands. In males large quantities of androgens (including testosterone) and in females oestrogen and progestins are released. Females enter puberty and mature on average two years earlier than males. In girls the growth spurt coincides with genital development. In boys genital development is almost complete before the growth rate accelerates. Around the age of 14, both sexes are of equal height, after which boys and men are taller. The psychologist, Helen Bee[6] has summarised male/female differences in a convenient form, reproduced in Table 2.4. Within each sex there are early and late maturers.

Table 2.4: Pubertal development

Characteristic	Average age (years)	Range of normal ages (years)
Boys		
Beginning accelerated growth of testes	11½	9½–13½
Beginning accelerated growth of penis	12½	10½–14½
Period of most rapid increase in height	13½	12½–17
Full development of penis	14½	12½–16½
Full development of testes	15	13½–17
Girls		
Breast buds	10½	8–13½
Axillary hair (e.g. underarm)	10½	8½–13
Pubic hair, beginning	11	9–13½
Period of most rapid increase in height	11	9½–14½
First menstruation	12½	10½–15½
Full breast development	13½	10½–18
Full pubic hair development	13½	10½–17

Source: Bee[6]

By the time the process of maturation and growth is complete, men are on average four inches taller than women. A higher proportion of the male body is muscle: 40 per cent as compared with 24 per cent in women. A female body contains proportionally more fat cells: 25 per cent as compared with 12 per cent of the male. Male lungs have 50 per cent bigger capacity than female. It has been found that training and exercise can alter these proportions, and male and female athletes can look alike. Women have a better chance of survival in so far as they replace blood faster, use up less oxygen and have a greater reserve of fat.

There is little controversy about physical differences, except the effect of training on potential. It is in the sphere of feelings and behaviour that the greatest controversies appear. From the moment of birth babies of both sexes enter into a complex process of interaction with those who care for them, and a chain of responses is set in motion. The notion of parents doing things to their children and vice-versa is an outmoded idea.

The newborn baby is invariably handed to the mother, unless she is unconscious. The father stands by even if he is present. On leaving hospital the baby is usually in its mother's arms; the father carries the suitcase. From the moment of birth the infant begins to absorb the idea that mothers and fathers play different roles, and has embarked on a lifelong process of socialisation – a process which is designed to help him/her fit into the culture and society into which s/he is born. White and lemon are 'neutral' colours, girls are adorned in pink frills, while 'blue for a boy' is still regarded as a norm. I doubt whether I would dare to buy a frilly dress for a friend's newly born boy, and may take the coward's way out, choosing a functional white outfit.

From birth onwards, although parents usually love children of either sex equally, they behave towards them in different ways. Girls are smiled at more frequently and soothed. Boys are played with more roughly. Restlessness in boys is interpreted as wanting to play, in girls as asking to be soothed. Mothers play and stimulate girls more than boys; the reverse is true of fathers. Different sets of adjectives are used to describe girls and boys, masculine and feminine traits of strength or sweetness being attributed from an early age. Infants grow up in different surroundings with different decor, a girl's nursery is likely to have more frills and pretty things than a boy's. While early playthings are the same, cuddly toys and floating animals are gradually replaced by construction toys for boys and replicas of domestic appliances for girls. The choice is made by parents and others bearing gifts. From the toddler stage onwards children are encouraged to behave in an appropriate way: girls to look pretty and not get too dirty, boys to be brave and explore.

The emotional environment of boys and girls is also different. During the first year of life all babies become attached to one or more preferred figures, who ensure the child's safety and comfort. Proximity is maintained through a number of behaviours such as sucking, smiling, crying, clinging and following. The caretaker responds to this and if s/he does not the behaviour, at least for a time, continues. Attachment is at its height during the last quarter of the first year and sets the pattern for other attachments in later life. Whereas originally Bowlby,[12] the founder of attachment theory, placed great emphasis on attachment to the mother figure, he later acknowledged (personal communication) the importance of fathers and his original ideas have been expanded by others.[93,97,98] A child can become attached to more than one person, who need not be female. Most children originally spend more time with their mother than with their father; boys have the difficult task of becoming like father, who is a more distant figure than mother. This could account for the difficulties many men have in expressing feelings and acknowledging dependency in themselves, as well as responding to feelings and dependency needs in their children and partners. Women are expected to act as carers. Boys' dependency on their mothers results in a lifelong search for a giving mother figure.

In the course of evolving gender identity as a part of self-concept, children have to master three basic tasks, and this usually happens in the same sequence. Firstly, they see themselves as either a boy or a girl. Secondly, they learn about gender stereotypes in the society of which they are a member. Thirdly, from a wide repertoire of possible behaviours they choose a range which forms their own pattern. It is likely that all these tasks are achieved in a variety of ways, and the major theoretical explanations can all contribute to the understanding of the process, rather than being mutually exclusive. According to psychoanalytic theories, identification with the parent of the same sex is an unconscious process and comes about as a solution to the conflict created by wanting to be physically close to the parent of the opposite sex and having to renounce that wish within the family. However useful this explanation, it also needs a social dimension, as do all the others. The parent is not only a biological but a social being, who plays a variety of roles. Children, particularly girls whose mothers work, have a more positive and clear image of the adult female, and tend to appreciate individual differences to a greater extent than children whose parents follow a rigid pattern. The social learning theory explains repetition of behaviour by its consequences. Behaviour which is rewarded tends to continue, while ignored or punished actions become extinguished. This theory encompasses the concept of modelling: conscious imitation of chosen role models in the person's environment. Cognitive theory stresses the part played by the stages of cognitive development. Children must recognise themselves and others as being permanently male or female, before choosing whom and what to imitate. This last theory stresses the child's own role in monitoring and acquiring behaviour.

Awareness of biological sex manifests itself around the age of two, though at first the child may not realise that this is a permanent state of affairs. By four and a half, most children have acquired this knowledge and by six they realise that this permanency applies to men and women generally. By the age of two and a half, children's gender stereotypes include a repertoire of things boys and girls like to do.

> Girls like to play with dolls, like to help mother, like to cook dinner, like to clean house, talk a lot, never hit and say 'I need some help', boys to play with cars, help their fathers, build things and say 'I can hit you'.[7]

While at this age boys and girls like their own characteristics and put down those of the opposite sex, male characteristics are increasingly seen as more prestigious and desirable as children grow older, and by adults. Socialisation pressures are stronger on boys than girls, who are punished and admonished more frequently for sex-inappropriate behaviour and told not to behave like a sissy, while girls who are tomboys are tolerated or even encouraged. The rigidity of sex stereotypes fluctuates with age, stage of development and knowledge. For instance, young children have rigid ideas, while by the age of eight they have become more aware of individual differences and a variety of jobs which either a man or woman could do. Adolescents seem to have a great need to conform while evolving their own identity, and show intolerance of sex-inappropriate behaviour.

Extensive research has been done on stereotypes and their validity, and there seems to be overwhelming evidence that many assumptions are false. Such research was undertaken by Maccoby and Jacklin[63] in the 1970s and has continued. On the basis of thorough investigation of a great volume of often conflicting and not always reliable evidence, Maccoby and Jacklin came to the conclusion that beliefs about sex differences can be classified into three categories; those for which there is sufficient evidence, those which are unfounded and those for which there is insufficient evidence to make a judgement.

Table 2.5: Unfounded beliefs about sex differences

Girls are more 'social' than boys.
Girls are more 'suggestible' than boys.
Girls have lower self-esteem.
Girls are better at rote learning and simple, repetitive tasks, boys are better at tasks which require a higher-level cognitive processing and the inhibition of previously learned responses.
Boys are more 'analytic'.
Girls are more affected by heredity, boys by environment.
Girls lack achievement motivation.
Girls are auditory, boys are visual.

Sex differences that are fairly well established
Girls have greater verbal ability than boys.
Boys excel in visual–spatial ability.
Boys excel in mathematical ability.
Males are more aggressive.

Open questions: too little evidence or findings ambiguous
Tactile sensitivity.
Fear, timidity and anxiety.
Activity level.
Competitiveness.
Dominance.
Compliance.
Nurturance and maternal behaviour.

Source: Maccoby and Jacklin.[63]

The conclusions based on research into sex differences must take into account a number of things. Behaviour is often specific in a particular situation, e.g. while girls readily comply with the requests of adults they are no more ready to obey their peers than boys. There is little evidence in some areas simply because they have not been studied: it is only recently that father/child interaction has received detailed attention, while there have been many studies of mother/child interaction; therefore it would be difficult to judge if there is any difference. In the course of my clinical experience I found that questions about early development are usually addressed to the mother; therefore the assumption that she is the prime carer excludes the father.

Very recently, a British psychologist, Nicholson,[81] on the basis of extensive review of research and literature, suggested that although differences in behaviour do exist, most of them are induced by environmental pressures and the reality of the social, cultural and economic context. Nicholson concludes: 'We have not so far come across any evidence which forces us to accept that men and women must behave differently because they are different biologically.' This perspective is shared by me.

3
Similar or Different?

The men in the study were asked a number of specific questions about male/female differences and, in addition, contributed their own ideas in areas not included in the questionnaire. They were encouraged to state their own views and refer to gut reactions and feelings rather than to objective evidence and research findings. Specific questions related to intellectual functioning, feelings, interests and aptitudes. Many men also commented on the difference between the male and the female body, and how anatomy and physiology can influence mental processes, feelings and behaviour. Where differences were thought to exist, the men were encouraged to say what they considered to be the reasons for these. Their comments provide an interesting insight into male views on the respective contributions of mother nature and socialisation: the nature/nurture debate.

The 'study' men seemed to be equally divided between those who believe that men and women have the same intellectual potential and those who maintain that it is different. Opinions were divided on whether female intellectual processes such as thinking and problem-solving are the same. A variety of reasons were given to account for the differences when they are thought to exist. Bert (87, retired fireman, widowed) was the main spokesman for those who thought that there was an essential innate disparity.

> Men are stronger physically and stronger mentally, I don't know if you agree with this. We have a woman Prime Minister and look what a mess she has made of things. I suffer from emphysema and not long ago I went to my GP. He said he could not give me the medicine I used to have

on the NHS. I wrote to two Members of Parliament, still nothing happened, so the country is not run well. That is what a woman Prime Minister has done to me. Mr Healey would not have done it, would have made a better Prime Minister. Mrs Thatcher had a good education but being married to a millionaire, she does not understand the needs of the poor. I used to vote Tory, now I vote SDP.

Further discussion and questions about Bert's views and the distinction I tried to make between policies and personalities resulted in an even firmer confirmation that a man, any man, would have made a better job of running the country than a woman. Bert is influenced by his personal experiences and attributes his misfortunes and plight to female inferiority of vision and judgement. He was finally able to obtain the medicines he had been relying on for many years through 'the kindness of his GP who bent a few rules, he is a man'. Bert and many other men have been heavily influenced by personal experiences, and it is difficult to tell whether their views have been formed on the basis of these or whether experiences which confirmed strongly held views were selected to justify already existing notions.

Trevor (61, retired bank manager, married) believes that 'men are more rational, more logical in their thinking. Women get very emotional.' Many other men made similar remarks about man's ability to be more emotionally detached than women and female emotionality getting in the way of thinking clearly. Donald (73, actor, divorced) stated that 'women are as intelligent but sometimes emotions get in the way. Girls win quiz games. Something happens towards the end of school – not as many (as men) go to university. I wonder if love gets in the way?' Lionel (55, draughtsman, single) believes that the fact that men go out to work and women stay at home has an effect. 'There is not so much depth to female thinking. They (women) seem to be more superficial, men think more deeply about their work because it covers a greater period of their lives.' Because men think 'more deeply' in specific situations, Lionel generalises on the basis of this and extends this belief to other contexts. Ramah (19, unemployed, single) volunteered that 'men are a bit more clear-headed, not so emotional, have a better sense of direction (intellectually).' Jimmy's statement was brief and reflects his bewilderment: 'it is a bit of a mystery, they [women] think different'. Jimmy (28, unemployed, single) was educated in a special school and described himself as 'mentally slow'. He finds it difficult, he said, to communicate with girls generally and to know what they are thinking. He has never had a close female friend or a girlfriend. He was brought up by his mother, his father having died when Jimmy was very young, and Jimmy claims to have been very close to his mother and his sister.

A small number of men felt that women have superior reasoning powers. Murray (23, student, cohabiting) suggested that women are sometimes better able to solve a problem intellectually because 'women have better concentration'. He quoted himself as an example of what many men do: 'I keep fidgeting, keep getting up to get a cup of coffee or something.' Sanjay (32, taxi driver, married) expressed his views at some length:

> Mentally, women can take more punishment than men can; they can see further and deeper into the future, maybe not in business world but in the personal world. Women have the same intellect. It is just that in the past they have not been encouraged or allowed to use it in the same way as men.

A few men put forward the idea that men and women are equally intelligent, but women do not want to compete with men and do not want to appear to be intelligent in case they are thought to be unattractive: Alex (54, scientist, divorced) referred to several outstanding women such as Marie Curie and Kathleen Lonsdale, and thought it was a pity that 'women do not want to use their intelligence so as not to appear to be a "blue-stocking", they prefer to be a "flesh-coloured one"'.

The view that men and women solve problems differently, but each way has its advantages, was put forward by a number of informants, including Craig (17, catering assistant, single):

> Say a man and a woman have got a problem, a man will go straight towards it, a woman will think about it and she will sort out the pros and cons of doing this or doing that. She will think about it and not jump straight into it. If it is something that needs sorting out straight away, then you just need to jump in and sort it out straight away, a man can do it better, specially if it is a physical problem, but if it is emotional a woman can do it better, she would think about it more.

Barry (20, unemployed, single) believes that 'girls take longer to make a decision but in the end it is a better one'. The theme of men being more decisive than women, and making decisions more quickly than women, and women making sometimes better decisions on the basis of having considered many more aspects emerged as a strong and recurrent one. It was raised in relation to male and female reasoning generally and also with reference to specific work situations, which will be more fully analysed in the chapter on education and employment.

Strong egalitarian views were expressed by men such as Ranjeev (26, nurse, cohabiting). 'To say that a woman is less intelligent because a man's brain is bigger is a load of rubbish: so is an elephant's brain.' The idea of similar intellectual functioning was supported by others.

Some of those who thought that men and women had the same potential but there were differences, e.g. in achievement, attributed this to a variety of factors: 'Men and women are not born with different capacities, but they respond to different expectations, broadly speaking, men are more intellectual, women more caring and emotional' (Harold, 56, lecturer, separated). Hugh (37, lecturer, single) believes that due to socialisation, men think more pragmatically with a view to arranging things.

The idea of individual differences within the same sex was frequently voiced by the men who believe that stereotyping on the basis of sex is misleading. Alf (89, retired commercial traveller, widowed) believes in individual differences: 'some women, like men, are intelligent, some not so intelligent. It depends on education. Some come from a poor family and do not get it (education) and so are less intelligent.' According to Jacob (78, retired butcher, widowed), 'some women are more intelligent than some men'. Uncertainty was expressed by Clifford (64, clerk, single): 'I don't have any personal views but I think that the person's sex is a secondary matter.' After much reflection, Leroy concluded that 'it is all based on how children is brought up. I can be rational and stand aside, but the majority of men cannot, there is no difference.'

Feelings and the way in which they are expressed were seen as one of the most fundamental differences between men and women, as fundamental as the belief that fathers cannot care for and relate in the same way as mothers to a young baby. These two sets of beliefs often have the same root: the deep conviction that women were created to carry and give birth to children and *ipso facto* are, therefore, better at caring for children and all humanity. Although there was some disagreement about whether men and women are fundamentally capable of having the same feelings, there was almost universal agreement that men and women show and deal with their feelings differently. A few men thought that the range of male and female emotions is basically different. 'Women can be more caring, more concerned about children and other people, this encompasses a range of different emotions. They [women] are better at physical care because of this' (Graham, 45, married). 'Women are more loving, it is natural as part of their childbearing function' (Bob, 65, probation officer, single).

Alf has a consistent and firm view, in contrast to most men in this book, who seemed quite unsure and hesitant in expressing a view. According to Alf (89, retired commercial traveller, widowed):

> A woman looks at things in a different light to what a man does. A woman is happy when she is made a fuss of and protected. There are a few women who want to be boss. Women get more emotional than men do – have different feelings. You get bad news and a man takes it better than a woman. A woman gets easily upset. Men show their feelings differently, by giving things like a bunch of flowers. A woman shows her feelings by fetching up a family, looking after the house.

Alf was unable to tell me exactly what he considered to be 'male' and 'female' feelings, but his conviction that they were different was unshakeable.

It was the different intensity of feelings that was emphasised by some men. 'Girls are more sensitive and therefore show their feelings more' (Ramah, 19, unemployed, single). 'Men get their feelings quicker and they tend to run shorter distances. A woman's feelings run very deep. I can also have feelings, but maybe not so deep' (Sanjay, 32, taxi driver, married). Stanley (22, money dealer, single) described his surprise when he found out from his own experience, and from his friends, how emotional women are and how easily upset they get over small things: 'A woman goes away and has a really good cry, men have the same feelings but are better able to control them.'

There was general consensus that men and women, for a

variety of reasons, show their feelings differently, and this has different consequences for themselves and for others; sometimes these are far-reaching. According to Alex (54, scientist, divorced) 'when a man lets his emotions run away, they often go into destructive channels. He puts on his uniform and goes to war. The women think and worry about their menfolk who don't return'. Lionel, (55, draughtsman, single) also emphasised the destructive potential of men, when their feelings run high. 'Women are more afraid of aggression but become depressed instead of fighting and have more illnesses.' Female emotions are seen as creative and caring; male, when uncontrolled, cause devastation on a grand scale. In the personal sphere, men and women assign different importance to their feelings. According to Eamonn (59, social worker, divorced):

> Women operate at a much higher emotional level, it is difficult to verbalise it. Women live their lives on a high emotional plane, men are staid. There are, of course, cultural differences. Women organise their lives according to their emotions, live in relationships, working them out, whereas men take relationships for granted. Women actually sit down and think things through, men don't. When women love, their feelings are stronger. They love more and hate more.

Those who thought that men express their emotions more easily than women were in a minority, and they took into account a very limited range of situations. Ivor (65, retired clerk, divorced) thinks that women who want to be 'ladylike' conceal their emotions, particularly in the early stages of a relationship: 'They act like a shy wallflower expecting a bumblebee to settle on them.'

Social pressures were the most frequently given reason for men and women showing and dealing with their feelings in different ways. These pressures were often resented and seen as oppressive. (Craig, 17, catering assistant, single):

> Men hide their emotions. Women are more open about their feelings, men are sort of closed up about them. If a bloke wants to cry, he should be able to cry. If I was on my own I would cry, but if I was out with my mates having a drink, I wouldn't, no way; they would start laughing.

Brought up in a traditional culture, Ranjeev (26, nurse, cohabiting) gave an example of how he was conditioned not to cry, but over the years has managed to find his own way of acknowledging his sadness:

> I was not sure initially if men and women had different feelings. I now think it is upbringing. Take, for instance, crying. It is something that 'women do' but five years ago I cried when my father died and since then I have been much more sensitive and emotional. Society stops you from showing your true feelings. My uncles came over for my father's funeral and kept telling me 'be a man, don't cry'. Society makes men repress feelings, it makes women show them. I don't think it's nature.

One is tempted to ask at this point who and what is 'society' in this case, if not an unwritten agreement between the majority of men that crying is a sign of 'weakness' and that they must not appear 'weak', even if they are. Richard (19, unemployed, single) comments on how men deal with sadness.

> Men have to be angry instead of upset. The conditioning can bring something out, a reaction that is not a natural feeling. At school I did not learn how to be a human being, how to deal with feelings.

Those men who believe that all human beings have exactly the same feelings are well represented by Gerald (36, social worker, married). Because of his job, he meets people in all kinds of situations, including crisis, having to cope with unforeseen loss, illness, bereavement and financial stress, family disruption and having to adapt to all kinds of new circumstances. These people, of both sexes and all ages, have the same feelings.

> Some erupt, others let go in dribs and drabs, some act them out. Men tend to hold on to their feelings, need encouragement to talk about them. I express my own sadness through humour: the effect of conditioning.

Apart from the effects of social conditioning, another explanation was put forward by several men, who believe that hormones and the menstrual cycle exert a strong influence on mood. Trevor

(61, retired bank manager, married) has 'noticed' that 'women go more up and down and tend to be erratic, flare up more easily than men. It's instinctive, to do with hormones and the menstrual cycle.' A similar view was expressed by Keith (31, banker, single). Whereas at one time he was more inclined to deny his emotions, he now admits that he can feel very happy and at other times experience extreme rage. 'If my moods change without any obvious cause then women's must change even more because of chemical changes.' Keith believes that both men and women can behave irrationally.

> Men usually deny it [being irrational], women explain their behaviour by the 'time of the month' and the effect of menstruation. They are even able to predict how they are likely to act at any particular time of the month.

A sociological explanation was provided by Hugh (37, lecturer, single) for any apparent differences in how feelings are expressed:

> Women put more emphasis on emotion, not necessarily because they are more in touch with theirs but because being excluded from positions of power, this is a compensation. Men tend to bottle things up, they need to feel they are in charge of their feelings. Male and female feelings are channelled differently: how and where they are expressed.

Many men are aware that things have been changing and will continue to do so. Some regret this, others welcome the change and most express mixed feelings. Chris (29, banker, single) has met many women in his life. He has a sister, has had girlfriends and works alongside female colleagues. These are his words:

> More and more women are hard and more and more men are soft, though there are still women who get very upset. Probably, men feel as much but when a couple split up, the woman is more likely to show that she is upset, he might say 'I don't need her anyway'.

Chris feels that men and women should be given equal chances to succeed in whatever they choose to do. He has found that some women are 'very hard' both in business and personal relationships, and does not believe that hardness and aggressiveness is necessary for success. He prefers to deal with women who have nice manners and can be gentle as well as determined to succeed. His current girlfriend is a university student. He likes to deal with women on an equal footing. Harold (56, lecturer, separated) considers that men and women are equal. Since being separated from his wife he has looked after his young children on a daily basis. He regrets that the Woman's Movement has had some undesirable consequences:

> In their search for equality some women have denied their tender feelings. Women are in revolt and sometimes they reject the caring side of their personality, to the loss of themselves, the men they have relationships with and their children.

Looking into the future, Donald (73, actor, divorced) explains that:

> Men have to earn a living and cannot allow their emotions to get too much in the way. This may not be so in the future. It will be interesting to see what happens to women if they go on this path of independence. They may have to contain emotions and become more aggressive. Now men are more aggressive physically, though women can be aggressive verbally.

It is worth commenting that already 41 per cent of the labour force is made up of women. A few men felt that society belittles men by allowing women to be more expressive and open about themselves. For instance, Clifford (64, clerk, single) pointed out that he is:

> Always suspicious about what is said about the difference between male and female emotions, not because it is not true that women feel deeply, but because it belittles man's emotions. I think that women show emotions more and they can burst into tears which is a thing I could not do. It must be a tremendous relief.

A few men thought they would like to change places with a woman, if not permanently, then at least temporarily, to know what it is like from inside and to be able to 'let their emotions flow'. 'I had a lovely dream the night before I came here to talk to you . . . I dreamt that I was a woman', said Clifford.

The question about interests elicited basically four types of answers: most men thought there were two distinctive categories of interests due to socialisation. A small number believe that there is an innate tendency for men and women to be preoccupied with different things. Most men were not quite sure what accounts for the fact that different activities had varying degrees of attraction for males and females. Individual differences were also taken into account. Vince (30, nurse, cohabiting) discovered around the age of 14 that he was attracted to men, not women, and remembers going through a phase of wanting to play with dolls and so-called girls' toys. He likes cooking and has always been interested in it. He comes from the north of England and within his family his interest in 'girls' and 'female' pursuits was strongly discouraged, particularly by his father. He believes that basically everyone has the same potential, but upbringing plays a vital part in what people do. John (30s, commercial artist, married) suggests that 'boys are more technologically oriented not only because of parental encouragement but all sorts of subtle messages all around the child'. His own two and half year-old son plays with other boys and girls 'all equally boisterous, but the subtle pattern of different interests is already there'. Daniel (37, vicar, married) believes that different interests are encouraged and perpetuated through the set-up within the family: 'the woman usually takes up the main burden of child-rearing and housework. It has a dulling influence on her interests and tends to blot out intellectual pursuits. The difference is not innate.' Trevor (61, retired bank manager, married) is among those who hold the view that different interests are

> born into us over hundreds of centuries. Men like using their bodies, play football. Girls like sedentary things, men are more interested in 'macho' things. Men would feel cissyfied if they did needlework. It has been like this for centuries. In some interests there is no or little difference.

According to Alf (89, retired commercial traveller, widowed):

> Men talk about football and dog racing. Women talk about fashion and things like that, unless you go to a political meeting. Then you know what you are going to talk about.

Men, when they get together, talk more about politics than women. Men are more interested in politics – it is in their nature.

The idea that men are more 'physical' was echoed by many others, though they were not sure if physical strength was necessarily the reason, and recognised that things are changing and girls have become more involved in sport. 'Men are more physical, play football, darts, women play hockey, my sister does different things from me, it's upbringing' (Jonathan, 17, unemployed, single). The reason for women taking an interest in sports is given by Vipul (50, care assistant, married) as 'they go there to be with the men, not because they like the football'. According to Barry (20, unemployed, single) female interests are less boring than male. 'Men talk about boring things: like cars, football and drugs.' Harold's statement reflects male uncertainty about the source of differences:

> Men tend to become interested in technical and intellectual matters. It is not possible to tell if nature or nurture accounts for this. Women are interested in relationships, feelings, artistic forms of expression such as music, painting, decorating. They are encouraged to develop this side more than boys are. I have some doubts about the nature/nurture contribution and would like to explore it more.

Eamonn (59, social worker, divorced) whose partner recently died, used to share many interests with her as well as both doing things on their own. 'A man likes to go down to the pub and play darts, a woman likes gardening, goes to pottery, music and flower arranging classes.' Murray (23, student, cohabiting) emphasised 'the gregariousness of women and the solitary pursuits of men' like himself. While he can spend a whole day on his own fishing, women, according to his observations, have greater need for company, whatever they are doing, and their hobbies bring them into contact with others.

To support the view that essentially there are no differences the phrase 'brainwashing' was used by Richard (19, unemployed, single). He spends his time with a group of male and female friends, most of whom are unemployed and have rejected conventional social values. 'There is a group of ideal interests that people are meant to have. A lot of people do that, without thinking about it.' The importance of class and money was brought out by Hugh (37, lecturer, single).

> One has to differentiate by social class. In the upper class, there is no difference, its members can indulge in hobbies and holidays. In other classes there are differences. Women tend to be more interested in clothes than men. Within the same class there are status groups, for instance, academics have similar interests. The women I mix with have similar interests to mine. A woman academic has more common interests with me than she might have with a woman working as a secretary.

The changing scene is described by Craig and Sanjay. 'Men are more physical but over the last couple of years, women have decided "let's do something about it". Women are catching up in physical sports, things like that' (Craig, 17, catering assistant, single); and 'Women may be better at hockey and men at football because of physical strength but I have seen women playing all sorts of games. I don't see any harm in a girl wanting to play cricket or football. Women should be allowed to' (Sanjay, 32, taxi driver, married).

Traditionally, men and women have been regarded as possessing different aptitudes, and this belief was embodied in some of the comments, but not all, because a number of men in this study do not believe in a demarcation along sex lines. Jeremy, a sculptor, took me around his house, full of beautiful objects, which he himself had designed and made. These include models of boats, the construction of which requires attention to minute and intricate detail, as well as larger objects executed in metal and crystal. Jeremy is a tall man, with large hands which he held in front of me in a convincing gesture demonstrating that dainty, small hands are not necessarily more of an asset in producing dainty objects. However, the idea that the size of the hand does make a difference is firmly held by some men, like Ralph (50s, teacher, divorced). 'Women use their hands better, while men use their strength.' Female dexterity was used as justification for female 'excellence' in a variety of situations ranging from dusting dainty objects (which a man would be likely to drop) to typing. Another 'female' characteristic used to justify different aptitudes was patience. 'Women are more patient, also better at detaching themselves from what they are doing. In men, thoughts and actions go together' (Roland, 54, personnel officer, divorced). Dick (19, unemployed, single) stated that 'boys are mechanically minded, girls are better at sewing and knitting, because they are patient', and 'Women are better at jobs that need patience' was how Vipul (50, care assistant, married) summed up 'male' and 'female' endowment.

The mothering instinct is often assumed to exist and account for female 'superiority' at tasks which require devotion, caring and empathy and this belief underlines the views of Lionel (55, draughtsman, single).

> Women are particularly good at nursing, social work, in all kinds of caring professions. This is related to mothering. From the beginning boys and girls play different games.

According to Keith, women have better social graces and are good at repetitive work to do with servicing the customer, including the domain of high finance in which Keith operates.

> Women are good at dealing with other people, they are far more amiable and amenable . . . they give the impression far more that they are interested, whereas someone like me could give the impression that I could not care a damn.

The 'same aptitudes, individual differences lobby' is also well represented. 'All differences in aptitudes have been exaggerated. We want the sexes to conform to a preconceived pattern. I am not satisfied with this and keep an open mind' (Bob, 65, probation officer, single). Trevor (61, retired bank manager, married) who has three daughters, illustrated his belief in individual differences by telling me that his 'eldest daughter is very good at science, my middle daughter at everything and is also very imaginative and the youngest excels at getting on with people and common sense'.

Economic conditions and the pay structure to a large extent define what aptitudes are assigned to each sex. 'Female' occupations are more poorly paid than typically 'male'. 'Women went into a number of areas in the industry, for instance, in Japan, because they are supposed to be good at assembling things. I suspect it is the low pay which does not attract men' (John, 30s, commercial artist, married).

The desire for change, with some ambivalence, is expressed by Eamonn (59, social worker, divorced):

Women are very good at fiddly jobs, men lack patience. A woman will always see things through. Men are better at heavier work. When put in a position where they need to compete, men have the ability to fight harder. Men are competitive. Women are far more persistent. The women I have known have far more stickability. Men give up more easily, whereas a woman, if she is committed, will keep on until the bitter end. Women have had a hard deal, have been second class citizens, now they have got their act together and are prepared to fight.

Individual informants offered comments on areas which they felt did not fall neatly under any particular theme, and of necessity many areas are not included in this book. One of the themes which emerged is aggression. Opinions were divided on whether men and women are equally aggressive. There was agreement, however, that if women did not fight physically as much as boys and men, they could be equally or more aggressive verbally. Comments about female soldiers not being 'born to kill' were offset by examples of bravery and aggression by female soldiers in countries where women fight alongside men.

Anatomical and physiological differences were often emphasised, and whereas male hormones and their possible influence were disregarded, female hormones were given great prominence. They were thought to have a variety of effects. These included mood swings, irrational behaviour, the desire to nurture and preference for doing housework rather than paid work outside the home, and feeling generally happier in domestic surroundings. What women and men generally do, and are expected to do, was often equated with a strong desire to actually do it.

Cleanliness was a quality attributed to women to a greater extent than to men. Women were said to be cleaner in relation to their bodies as well as their environment. There seemed to be agreement that 'men do not see dust' and women not only are better at cleaning, but also like it better than men. The way the sexes view each other was described by Simon (27, unemployed, single) as 'a game':

> When men get together they put women down, when women get together they probably put men down. It is all part of the game. Women to some blokes are like another drug, to be used. It's more like beer. They talk as though

they [women] were possessions, some mean it, some don't. It is all society. It's a load of rubbish. You are in a pub, but if you are on your own you are different. It is something already there. It is accepted. You accept other people's opinions. It is on the telly and idiots believe it.

In the face of strongly held conviction by some men that differences are due to social conditioning, and that there are large individual differences between persons of the same sex, the following statement is highly controversial:

Man is an inventor, doer, improviser, seeker after better things. Women maintain status quo. A woman would not put herself to trouble to look for a better method. A man is prepared to 'rock the boat', women want to maintain an equilibrium. Man is an analyser, a dissector and then he puts it together. He takes risks. Men and women are complementary. A boy will play with soldiers, put them into positions, without any egging on from his parents.
(Alex, 37, scientist, divorced.)

Since my main object in writing this book is to take a risk and 'rock the boat' should I at this point give up gracefully?

4
Education

Compulsory education begins for all children at the age of five, and most adults profess to believe that boys and girls should have the opportunity to study the same subjects. In one recent large scale survey,[55] 96 per cent of those questioned subscribed to this belief, and in another about 80 per cent.[71] In reality, boys and girls are treated very differently during their pre-school years as well as during the 16,000 hours the average child spends at school. The two sexes experience a different set of expectations and treatment from their parents, teachers, peers and the media. Their own self-image and behaviour differ considerably throughout the school years, culminating in highly unequal numbers and uneven distribution between the subjects studied in further and higher education. Research into sex differences indicates that baby boys and baby girls are born with similar aptitudes and abilities, and that the differences between individuals of the same sex are as great as the differences between the sexes. The only differences which seem to be biologically influenced are spatial perception and mathematical ability.

Early learning takes place in a variety of ways. When children behave spontaneously and play such games as hiding their faces and peeping out in a flirtatious manner, girls are more likely to be rewarded for this than boys. Toys are a good example of differential treatment. While all babies start off playing with rattles, floating animals and cuddly toys, as they grow older the pressure towards different type of play increases. Toy shops have been found to have separate sections for boys', girls' and family toys.[28] Among boys' toys are weapons, construction toys and spaceman outfits. Among girls' toys, dolls, prams and miniature domestic appliances predominate. Family toys include books, jigsaws and board games. Boys' toys encourage exploration and early application of analytical thinking and science. Girls are steered into acquisition of social and nurturing skills. Boys play with models of objects, girls with dolls which symbolise people. By the age of five boys have already been better prepared for a scientific career. Parents are more likely to buy a computer for a son than a daughter, and girls who have a brother have access to a computer more frequently than girls who are only children or have sisters only.

> There is an increasing body of evidence to suggest that lack of early activities involving spatial awareness, and insufficient experience with mechanical toys and puzzles, are important contributory factors in the later underachievement of girls in mathematics and science.[29a]

All pupils study the same subjects in most primary schools. However the Equal Opportunities Commission (EOC) has found that some schools still provide an opportunity for boys only to sample a range of crafts, and for girls to begin learning needlework and sewing. 'The different treatment of boys and girls in primary schools is a subtle process . . . The subtlety . . . does not diminish its power: attitudes learned early often persist'.[29a] Boys are provided with mechanical things, and encouraged by teachers to explore them, whereas a girl's interest may remain unnoticed, as often is the case with unexpected behaviour, thus reinforcing the power of stereotypes: behaviour which is expected is more likely to be noticed. In psychological experiments people who are shown pictures of green donkeys and brown leaves, usually say that they had seen pictures of brown donkeys and green leaves. The books which are used during the early stages of learning often portray boys and men in exciting situations, exploring outer space, having mastery over people and environment and engaged in 'male' occupations. Girls and women are often portrayed as helpless, caring for other people and in typically 'female' jobs such as a nurse or typist.

Teachers claim that they treat boys and girls in similar ways. Surveys reveal that this is not always so. Teachers often assume that girls learn because they are diligent and try to please, while boys may be less attentive but academically more able. One group of teachers described girls as: obedient, tidy, neat, conscientious, gossiping, orderly, fussy, catty and bitchy, whereas boys were said to be: lively, adventurous, aggressive, boisterous, self-confident, independent, energetic, 'could not care less' and loyal (*Sexism in schools*, Association of Educational Psychologists, quoted in Ref 29). Teachers tend to spend more time with boys, if only to control them, but also to encourage them to solve problems and succeed. Boys receive more praise and more criticism than girls. By the end of their primary education most pupils 'have learned to live with the prejudices and ideas of society and have accepted their place in it'. This conclusion is reached by the Equal Opportunities Commission and carefully documented in its publication: *Girls and Information Technology*[29] which reports on a research project carried out jointly with the Croydon Local Education Authority (LEA) set up in 1983, the year designated as Women into Science and Engineering (WISE). Croydon had set up three-year courses in information technology for all pupils aged 11–14, and the project looked at the progress of this venture. Some of the findings are generally applicable and of great interest.

On entering secondary education, boys and girls brought with them strongly held views about supposed male superiority in science subjects and the 'most strongly sexist attitudes were held by boys aged 14'. Many girls complained that they felt the subject of information technology was dominated by boys: boys were more vocal, girls felt intimidated, boys received more encouragement from teachers and textbooks reflected typically male interests. When an effort was made by teachers to give extra encouragement to girls they responded favourably, and open discussion in mixed groups partly eradicated prejudice. In a Croydon girls' school, option choices were found to be highly affected in the direction of choosing computer studies and information technology by good and enthusiastic teaching.

In mixed classes it has been found that boys do better than girls in mathematics and science subjects, the reasons given by girls being that they feel generally intimidated as well as embarrassed by the sexual remarks and attention which is paid to them by boys. Pat Mahoney,[65] as a result of her survey of coeducational secondary schools, comes to the conclusion that boys, rather than girls, benefit from coeducation, which prepares them for segregated adult roles.

At the stage when pupils have to choose their fourth year options the choice has been usually already determined, not only by ability but by stereotypes. Not enough is done by those who advise children on their choices to encourage a wide range of

Education

Table 4.1: GCE 'O' and 'A' level passes, 1984, England and Wales

(females as percentage of all passes)

Subject	CSE (grade 1)	'O' level	'A' level
Technical drawing	5.6	5.1	3.1
Physics	20.8	27.6	21.0
Mathematics	48.7	43.8	30.0
French	69.2	61.1	73.8
Domestic subjects	96.6	97.4	99.2

Source: EOC[30]

subjects and suggest that pupils consider areas which are typically seen as paired with the opposite sex. That does not mean that individual parents or teachers do not do all they can and offer impartial advice. An 'open' choice is sometimes predetermined by a previous choice which had already been made, as in the case of a school which offered technical drawing to all pupils, but made it a condition that it had to be paired with metalwork, which had previously been offered to boys only.

Examination results at 'O' and 'A' levels of GCE can be gleaned from the Department of Education and Science publications, and recently have been studied locally, e.g. in Humberside.[46] The pattern for boys is different from that for girls. More girls than boys enter for 'O' levels, but fewer for 'A' levels. In 1984, girls obtained 53.6 per cent of all CSE grade 1 passes, 51.2 per cent of GCE 'O' level passes and 47 per cent of GCE 'A' level passes. Overall, the pass rate for boys was lower than girls at CSE level, similar at 'O' level and higher at 'A' level. Girls predominate in arts and languages, and boys in science, technical drawing and computer studies. Table 4.1 illustrates segregation of boys and girls according to subjects. Of those who left school with CSE or 'O' level passes, more girls than boys went into further education: mostly into secretarial courses, while more boys decided to look for a job. Of those who left school with at least two 'A' level passes, more than two-thirds continued in full-time education. More boys (58 per cent) than girls (46 per cent) went on to degree courses.

In further education, men predominate on advanced courses (60.9 per cent) and women on non-advanced ones (53.7 per cent). On science, engineering and technology courses men are the majority, while women study on arts, education, health and welfare courses. Although the number of women on full-time engineering and technology courses has increased, it has only reached 6.6 per cent of the total number of students taking these subjects. Among university undergraduates women constitute less than half of the total number (31.8 per cent) and women predominate on language, music, drama and education courses.[30] Men and women have very different preparation for life and employment within the educational system which has, until recently, quite openly prepared men for paid work and women for domesticity, and more recently prepares women for a dual role of paid worker and housemaker. The 1944 Education Act and the Sex Discrimination Act 1975, have laid the foundations of equality, but only a change of attitudes can bring about their true implementation.

> The wastage of talent and opportunity among both sexes in education is undeniable. It is difficult to challenge the prevailing orthodoxy. It can take courage for a boy to show a serious commitment in home economics at school, just as it does for a girl to insist on becoming an engineer.[90]

Education, as was pointed out quite rightly by one informant, 'is a 24-hour thing. It goes on at school, in institutions of further and higher education, at home. By the time a child starts going to school they have already had a lot of education' (Benjamin, 43, clerk, divorced). My own questioning about education was confined to the more formal process, and I wondered if boys and girls should be not only allowed but encouraged to study the same subjects, whether parents should give any priority based on sex – if financial resources are scarce – in helping their children to stay on at school beyond 16. I was interested in the men's own educational experience and whether they themselves had ever witnessed discrimination, in whatever form.

There was almost universal agreement that boys and girls should study the same subjects, and a variety of reasons were given for this. Those in their late 70s, 80s and 90s, were divided in their views. The youngest men were able to comment on their own experience from a distance of only a few years, and a small number of men produced examples of subtle and not so subtle differential treatment and behaviour. Only two men openly pronounced themselves in favour of treating boys and girls differently. Apart from these two, even those men who believe in highly segregated roles in life surprisingly 'did not mind' girls doing metalwork and boys learning about cookery, as long as married women did not use their 'male' skills to compete with men in the field of paid employment, and stayed at home to look after their families, always putting their husbands and children first.

Alf (89, retired commercial traveller, widowed) expressed a deeply felt conviction that 'women's work is women's work and men's work is different. Men and women do different things in life and should be prepared for this at school. There is no point in boys doing cookery and girls metalwork.' Dick (19, unemployed, single) informed me that although there are

> some general subjects, there are also masculine and feminine things. I would want my son to learn mechanical things and my girl also, but not to the same level. If a boy wanted to learn how to knit I would not stop him but I would not be pleased. I would encourage a girl more.

Even those who seem to hold the view that boys and girls should study the same subjects excluded knitting and child care. If a school offers tuition in these, it was thought that boys should be excused if they did not want to partake. Female 'nature' and future maternal role were given as justification for child care, also that boys might drop the baby (doll). No reason was given for excluding knitting.

Most of those in their teens and early 20s and two of the eldest men, expressed general dissatisfaction with the educational system, for different reasons. Jacob, aged 78, is 'generally horrified' at what goes on at school, particularly boys and girls learning together about sex. He believes it is up to the parents to educate their children about these matters when the right time comes. To prove his point he quoted in detail several cases of schoolgirls becoming pregnant, which had been reported in the press. He blames today's education and lack of parental supervision for all of the contemporary evils, including poor moral standards.

The younger men expressed dissatisfaction ranging to anger and disgust for a different set of reasons. Those who went to single-sex schools described these as a very unnatural environment.

'Meeting girls later, after leaving school, was a culture shock, but a good one' (Barry, 20, unemployed, single). He now believes that people are individuals and should be respected as such. Until he met some girls in his late teens he thought of girls as strange creatures, 'did not know how to treat them'. Another strong opponent of single-sex schools and the education system generally is Richard (19, unemployed, single). He said:

> I don't agree with the education system anyway. I don't think it does children any good. You look at them before they go in and they run around smiling. Years later they don't. The teachers are shouting at them, using ideas that are their (teachers') own. It makes you a nervous wreck. The last few years I was in a school where boys and girls were kept in separate buildings. It really messed me up. I came out of that school feeling that I could not talk to women, they were a different species. It made me shy and self-conscious. Boys were encouraged to play football, get into the cricket team, not home economics. Girls played hockey. This is very wrong.

The belief that boys and girls should be treated in exactly the same way was strongly subscribed to by men of all ages, including two of the eldest, who think things have changed for the better and wish they had as good an education as young people today. The following selection of quotes illustrates the sentiments of the majority of the men in the book: 'It may well be that boys and girls could be interested in different subjects, but that should be left to find its own level. I don't think that boys should be encouraged to take one direction and girls another' (Clifford, 64, clerk, single). Alex (54, scientist, divorced) advocates:

> Up to the age of 16 boys and girls should have the same grounding in the common skills: linguistic, arithmetic and humanities, including home economics. It does not do boys any harm to learn to cook and sew. In higher education the parameter must be aptitude and this is individual. In the Soviet Union there are almost as many lady engineers as men.

Sydney (52, book-keeper, divorced) confided: 'I cannot cook, but if girls wish to do woodwork and boys cookery, why not?' Hugh expressed his regret at not having taken domestic science at school and made up for it since, while he fully shared all domestic chores with his cohabitee. Troy (58, retired scientist, divorced) thought that 'if parental financial resources were scarce, they should divide them equally between their children and encourage them all equally, regardless of sex, to have a good education' of which Troy himself has had the benefit. Both the teachers, Ralph and Graham strongly advocate equal opportunities for boys and girls and positive encouragement to consider a range of subjects, since such encouragement is necessary to offset prejudice and opting for subjects not on the basis of ability but preconceived ideas. Vipul gave a slightly different reason for girls needing a good education: being weaker than men physically they need the benefit of a good education to protect them and give them an equal chance in life. He will encourage his own daughter to go to university.

Several instances were given of boys and girls being treated differently. Although it is not long since Murray left school — only five years — he remembers that girls were not allowed to do woodwork or metalwork and boys to do cooking. In spite of this background, he and the young woman he lives with share domestic chores. Ramah (19, unemployed, single) remembers that 'boys used to get shouted at a lot at my school . . . boys do not have much patience, they have to be pushed harder. Girls apply themselves more, boys mess around.' Differential treatment was also referred to by Adam (21, unemployed, single): 'Boys used to be treated more harshly, teachers used to raise their voices. Girls got shouted at less for the same thing. Teachers let them off.' Sanjay (32, taxi driver, married) comments on discrimination:

> the way teachers teach boys and girls is different. They [teachers] pay more attention to boys. In India it is the other way round. There are fewer girls at school, there were six girls and twenty boys in my class, so girls got most of the teacher's attention.

Daniel (37, vicar, married), whose son brings home knitting from school, commented that he was not sure if letting girls have a go on the computers and boys at knitting goes far or deeply enough to combat subtle discrimination. Graham, a headmaster, also commented on subtle forms of treating boys and girls differently. 'A great deal of talk goes on in the staffroom' which reflects deeply embedded attitudes and expectations which may not be reflected in the curriculum. Ranjeev (26, nurse, cohabiting) gave examples from his nursing training:

> Male nurses were expected to do better than female. As far as I am concerned, I am Mr Average. The majority of tutors tend to be male . . . it pays more. They would naturally be favourable toward male student nurses, ask them difficult questions, so they could show off if they knew the answer. Everyone would say 'wow, that was a difficult question'.

Two older men, each of whom has daughters, described how they defied social conventions and succeeded in 'male' subjects. One of Karmi's daughters is a doctor, the other has a degree in mathematics and physics and is now studying for a higher degree in astronomy. One of Roland's daughters is also a doctor and the other has a Higher National Diploma in business studies. These young women were encouraged by their fathers to disregard assumptions and social convention.

Examples were also given of schools where boys and girls were treated similarly, for instance by Craig (17, catering assistant, single), who went to a mixed school which he left 18 months ago. 'The girls did as much sport as the boys. Cookery in the second year was compulsory for all and girls did metalwork . . . if there was discrimination I must have been going around with my eyes closed.'

Many men commented that their own attitudes have changed, for instance Gerald. After leaving school, 17 years ago, he took an engineering course. He remembers only one girl among the male students. She was Indian and very slightly built. The men used to laugh and joke at her expense, and Gerald was among them. His views have changed, and he would not do so now.

An interesting insight was provided by Benjamin into his early upbringing in Ghana and how his own views have changed. In his school days girls did not have the same opportunities as boys, and it was thought to be a waste of time to educate a woman who would be tied to the kitchen sink for the rest of her life. As a single parent, who is bringing up his daughter, he spends a great deal of time helping and encouraging her not only to do well at school, but to find out as much as possible about a whole variety of things. He believes that 'people shape their environment' and hopes his daughter will shape hers.

Education

Keith, who has had an Oxbridge education, remembered that his female contempories were 'very clever, some a lot cleverer than many men and worked a lot harder, it was almost as though they had something to prove' (Keith, 31, banker, single).

5
Employment

One of the questions asked was about work which is paid for: whether men and women are capable of doing the same type of work, whether they should receive equal pay for doing work of equal value and whether they have achieved equality in this sphere. I explained that in this context 'work' meant working for a financial reward either as an employee or being self-employed. A separate question was asked about housework and looking after children and these merit separate chapters to themselves. The word 'work' often conjures up an image of work which carries with it financial reward, in spite of the fact that housework and child care can mean a much longer and harder day than eight hours spent in an office or a factory. Also it is hardly ever recognised, and certainly not in official statistics, that some paid jobs could not be done without the backup of the partner who services, in a variety of ways the person who 'goes out to work'. Feminist writers, for instance, Oakley and Oakley[83] have pointed out that official statistics such as those collected for and quoted in the Census and New Earning Survey are geared to the kind of work men do, rather than women. For instance, those who work for money at home, home machinists, child minders, mail order representatives are exclusively female. The 1981 Census was the first one to include a question about homeworkers. The New Earnings Survey does not include low earners who do not pay income tax through the PAYE system. These low earners are made up mostly of women, working part-time. The doctor's wife, who answers his telephone, or the builder's daughter who types his invoices is not officially a member of the 'labour force'.

The exclusion of many working women from the labour force is a reflection of an ideology which sees man as the breadwinner

Employment

and his female mate as mother and homemaker. In Victorian times a woman who did not conform to the idea of an 'angel in the house' was an embarrassment to be swept under the carpet. The idea has survived, although increasingly with less wholehearted support, and viewed with some ambivalence. Many men are like Stanley (in his 20s) who has no objection to his future wife working as it will mean a higher standard of living, but also would feel proud if she did not have to work and he could support her.

Yet women, like men, have always worked. In pre-industrial England the wife's occupation tended to be determined by the husband's. His trade was regarded as the chief source of income and he had authority over his wife, children and any servants which the household included. The wife had the main responsibility for the household and children. The work which she did was usually done in the company of other women. The process of industrialisation has resulted in a sharp division between home – where people eat, sleep, bring up children – and the workplace such as the office and the factory. Handicrafts were replaced by mass-made goods, and collective working at home was replaced by women working at home in isolation or alongside other women in mills and factories, such as the textile mills in Lancashire and silk weaving factories in Essex and Norwich. In rural areas, both men and women worked in the fields. Certain occupations, such as clerical, became designated as male – the 1851 Census did not list any female clerks. From 1830s onwards concern about women in factories working under bad conditions has resulted in the notion of a 'family wage': the man being able to earn sufficient money to support his family. This concern has had a double-edged effect: it is beneficial to women but also, for more than a century, resulting in lower pay and women being treated as male dependents in the Welfare State.

Currently, the 'workforce' is made up of 41 per cent women and 59 per cent men.[21] In June 1985 the estimated numbers in employment were 11.5 million men and 9.3 million women. The number of self-employed persons was 2.6 million approximately, of whom 75 per cent were men.[30] In a recent survey[71] 90 per cent of men and 69 per cent of women were described as 'economically active', i.e. either employed or seeking work. Between 1983 and 1985 male unemployment remained at a fairly steady level, while female employment increased by almost half a million.[30]

The pattern of working lives for men and single women is

different from that of married women and again from married women with young children.[71] Most men and single women work full-time between completing their education and retirement, unless ill or unemployed. Most married women work part-time but those with young children usually give up work and stay at home until the youngest child starts school. If only one of the couple works it is usually the husband. This was found to be so in 31 per cent of all couples. In 2 per cent of couples the wife worked while the husband stayed at home, and in 57 per cent of couples, both worked.

On marriage, few women give up work completely, but often change to part-time employment. About 60 per cent of married women without children, and 70 per cent of those with children, work part-time. Only a small minority of mothers (4 per cent) have an uninterrupted career, usually those who are well educated and have well-paid jobs. Most women give up work when the first child is born and return to work temporarily between births and permanently when the youngest child is 16. Those whose youngest child was born between 1975 and 1979 on average returned to work within three and a half years, and of those who completed their families in the 1960s, 90 per cent returned to work eventually. The proportion of mothers who go out to work increases with the age of the youngest child, as does the proportion of those who work full-time.

Many women, unless they return to work immediately, experience downward mobility, in terms of pay and careers, while men continue to work and move upwards. On return to work only one-third of women receive the same pay and stay in a job which is the same or comparable with the previous one. Half move downwards, particularly part-timers.

For married men, the presence of children results in more working hours in paid employment, especially those on a low wage.[94] For men in occupations with a career structure the pressure to climb the ladder coincides with the time when the children are young.[113] Single fathers, with responsibility for dependent children, find themselves in the same situation as married and single mothers: they have to adjust their working hours, travelling distance, responsibilities at work and take time off. Their career prospects are adversely affected.[39]

Within the whole field of employment there remain very few formal and legal mechanisms which allow discrimination between men and women: a woman is not allowed to work underground in a coalmine, in a lighthouse and on a North Sea oil rig. There are, however, many less tangible rules resulting in what has been described as vertical and horizontal segregation.[71] 'Vertical' refers to men and women being clustered in different occupations, 'horizontal' to men predominating in those which are more desirable. In the WES survey, most men (81 per cent) and women (63 per cent) said that they work alongside their own sex only. Male occupations seem to be more highly 'one sex only', than female. A list of selected occupations and proportions of men/women employed in them is given in Table 5.1.

Table 5.1: *Occupational segregation*

Men predominate	Men (%)	Women (%)
Construction, mining, related	96.6	0.4
Transport operating, materials moving, etc.	95.4	4.6
General management	89.8	10.2
Women predominate		
Catering, cleaning, hairdressing and other personal services	24.1	75.9
Clerical and related	26.3	73.7
Professional and related in education, welfare and health	32.0	68.0

Source: Ref. 30

In most prestigious professions men outnumber women. In 1985, according to an EOC report, men constituted 73 per cent of the membership of the British Medical Association, 86 per cent of the Law Society and 93 per cent of the Institute of Chartered Accountants. In 1968, the *Directory of Directors*, which covers 1500 UK companies, lists 1500 women (2.9 per cent of total membership).[30] In Parliament women now hold 6 per cent of seats following the 1987 General Election.

Predominantly male occupations are better-paid than female, and offer a better career structure. Within many occupations men hold better-paid positions, e.g. in primary schools there are four times as many female teachers as male. In the secondary sector, where salaries are higher, men predominate. Headmasters of schools, heads of departments and university professors are usually male.[21]

There is a great deal of stereotyping attached to different jobs.

Employment

Table 5.2: Occupational stereotypes

	Particularly suitable for men (%)	Particularly suitable for women (%)	Suitable equally (%)
Traditionally male occupations			
Car mechanic	72	1	25
Bus driver	49	1	49
Police officer	49	*	49
Bank manager	39	1	58
Traditionally female occupations			
Secretary	1	60	38
Nurse *	*	41	47
Political, service or newer occupations			
Member of Parliament	16	*	82
Local councillor	12	1	85
Social worker	1	11	87
Family doctor/GP	10	1	87
Computer programmer	6	3	89

Source: Witherspoon[112].

Many female jobs are seen as an extension of the woman's caring role at home: it is though quite legitimate for a female to mind not only her own, but other people's children, to teach infants, to nurse, service her boss as a personal assistant and care for the customer, if possible, combining professional skills with visual attractiveness. Table 5.2 contains a list of stereotypes.

Men and women give different reasons for seeing particular occupations as being mainly 'male' or 'female'. Women think that there are certain jobs which a man *would* not do because the jobs are boring or badly paid. Men claim that there are jobs which a woman *could* not do because the work is skilled, too heavy and the working conditions too unpleasant.[71] Certain heavy jobs appear to be attractive to some men because of their 'macho' image.

Most men and women work for the same reason: they need money for necessities. More men than women see themselves as working mainly for money. There is also a discrepancy between the value that working wives and their husbands place on the wife's job: more wives see their job as essential for the family's standard of living. Helen Franks, who spoke to a large number of men in this country and the USA,[34] came across a significant number who trivialised their wife's work. She coined the word 'jobettes' to described how some men rated their wives' jobs. What is often overlooked is that the majority of people enjoy going out to work, and would continue doing so even if they did not need the money.[112]

About a third of the population are still traditionalistic in their attitude and believe that the husband should be the main breadwinner and the wife should stay at home. A high proportion believe that mothers with children under five should be with them.[71,112]

The Legislation of the 1970s – the Equal Pay Act 1970 and the Employment Protection Act 1975 – embody the principle of equality. Since 1984 the Equal Pay Act has encompassed not only 'same' work but also work of 'equal value'. The Employment Protection Act ensures six weeks' maternity pay and reinstatement at work of women who qualify. Almost everyone seems to be in favour of equal pay and non discrimination at work.[71,112] In spite of the egalitarian measures and expressed views, equal pay has not been achieved. The gross hourly female earnings are just over half of male.[21] As a 1975 Government Paper[49] points out: 'the causes of continued inequality are complex and rooted deeply in tradition, custom and prejudice'.

The men in the study hold a variety of views ranging from those who believe men and women are totally interchangeable in the sphere of paid work to those who emphasise that there are only some jobs which can be done equally well by both sexes. The majority favour equal pay and treatment at work. The few who do not were an exception. A range of reasons were given both to justify equality and discrimination. Neither age nor occupation seemed to determine views, with the exception of those aged 80 and over, who firmly stated that a woman's place was in the home, regardless of what else she was capable of. Even the eldest men, as were most of the others, were often expressing what seemed to be contradictory views, both saying that males and females were and were not interchangeable as employees. This is not surprising in the face of new legislation and changing beliefs not accompanied by much real change.

The eldest four men expressed their uncertainty more openly than the others. According to Alf (89, retired commercial traveller, widowed):

> Women should do 'women's' work. A woman's place is not to run a business but to stay at home, but if a woman wanted

to she could do the same work as a man, instead of staying at home and settling down. If a woman has the capability and good education she could even be a bank manager. It is all right for a woman to work if it is to provide extra comforts for the family, not if she does it to buy extra clothes for herself. There are a few ambitious women who want to run the men. A woman would make a good commercial traveller, but a better nurse. A man would not make a good nurse, a man does not think another man should be ill and would expect him to get better the next day. He would not have the patience to give him his medicines and dress his wounds. In my days, when a girl got married, that was the end of her working life. Today I would not mind being driven by a woman bus driver, as long as she has passed her exams.

Jacob (78, retired butcher, widowed), also thinks that women can now do most jobs men used to do, because 'women have become more intelligent'. Whether they should is another matter. Jacob has recently read in the paper about a case which confirmed his belief in female domesticity as an ideal. 'This woman came home from work and found her husband in bed with another man, men cannot control their . . . you know what.' Presumably, if the wife had been at home she could have watched over her husband's morals. Having so justified women's domestic role, Jacob went on to say:

A woman can do any job a man can, they had to when men were in the army. There were lots of women butchers. Now they work as cashiers, they may serve you with a steak or a chop from the window. It is all right for a woman to fly a plane, but not to America – that is too tricky; sorry, I would not personally trust a woman pilot. It is a tricky job and you have to know this and that, you have to be careful, specially the landing. Women should not be kept at home like prisoners. They are good at putting things together in factories, like TV sets. I would not mind seeing a woman doctor, some are very good, just like men. Woman can drive cars. In Israel they have women soldiers and they are trained to kill, just like the men are . . . even in Arab countries women have to fight. But I am not really in favour of women working. They should either be at home or out doing the shopping.

Employment

Bert (87, retired fireman, widowed) also subscribes to the 'angel in the house' ideal of a woman. 'If our present Prime Minister had conformed to this, we would not have had the Falklands disaster . . . women are neither built nor destined by nature to have responsibility.' I was given a detailed account of occasions on which Bert advised women to 'follow their true instinct' and not apply for top jobs and promotion which they did not really want. 'Why should they go against their nature?' The law of the jungle was finally quoted by Bert to convince me that 'it is the lion's job to protect the lioness'. 'I may be wrong' concluded Bert, 'but this is what I believe.'

Charlie (90, retired engineer, widowed) recalls how 'the wars opened up things for women' and it would be wrong to put the clock back. Women are now more educated.' Charlie would be quite happy to entrust his safety to a female pilot or bus driver, but regrets that female independence has resulted in more divorces. 'Women who are independent don't think twice about leaving their families.'

Keith (31, banker, single) believes that women do not make good money dealers because 'they do not cope well under stress, they either panic or they freeze, there are not many female money dealers in the City, but the ones there are are a lot better than most men.' Leroy (23, unemployed, single) feels protective towards women in emergency situations:

> A lot of women are 'trousers' women, against society and men. They can get on with any job but how frightened would they get if they work with an electric saw and the blade snaps. Could they overcome their emotion? They might get all scatty and wobbly. A man would grab the thing and throw it out of the window. I would run away. Men and women can both go to war. Men are less brave today than they were – their bravery went out in the evolution. A man would not necessarily cope better in an emergency. It is just the fear of putting a woman on a machine that is dangerous, the idea upsets me. I feel protective . . . a man could make as good a typist or nurse as a woman.

However, many men disagreed with that last statement, for instance Craig (17, catering assistant, single):

> If I was in an office typing, making one mistake after

another, I would go mad. A woman is more patient, more careful. Maybe some women could be a dustman, but most women like to take care of their appearance. There are only a few things a woman could not do: heavy labouring and be a soldier – she would question herself (more than a man) about the morals of killing someone. I have never seen an advert for a woman bus driver – I am sure a woman could do it.

The notion that women are good at repetitive work was one of the main themes which found supporters among those who emphasised differences. The chief protagonist seemed to be Alex (54, scientist, divorced) who voiced his strong conviction about physical and mental differences, having also said that men and women are interchangeable, except for physical strength, thus displaying some uncertainty:

> Women have dexterity, more nimble fingers. A woman can shut off from what she is doing, insulate herself. A man worth his salt could not shut himself off from the totality of his task, he has an enquiring mind. A woman can type 'gobbledy gook' and not stop to think. A man would stop to say 'it is a load of rubbish'. Women are good at monotonous assembly work.

Alex did admit that monotonous work is 'soul-destroying' and does not encourage thinking.

> Women are better at doing stupid jobs not because they are stupid, but they are better at excluding their environment, they accept stupid jobs better. It is due to training. There are not many male typists – my own secretary was a man, men can type. (Ivor, 65, retired clerk, divorced)

Other fundamental differences which were emphasised were that men are more brave and have a 'better head for heights', therefore, make better window cleaners and steeplejacks. The belief that men are better at science and women at caring also cropped up intermittently. Harold (57, lecturer, separated) expressed doubts about 'whether women are as suited as men to occupations which require very strong scientific or technical expertise' but was not sure of the reason for this. According to

Trevor (61, retired bank manager, married) 'women are better at teaching infants, because they have been doing that kind of work for centuries, better at caring for children. They are more patient and make good nurses.' Apart from female superiority as carers and tolerance of monotonous work, only Barry (20, unemployed, single) believes that 'women are better organised and think quicker than men'.

The currently employed men in manual occupations such as building, painting and decorating emphasised the difference between men and women in strength and agility. Frank and Darren, both specialising in roofing work, did not think it would be outside the realms of possibility for a woman to be able to do what they did, but she would find it harder to do the work, for instance, carry a heavy load of roof tiles up or down. Frank would not mind being a househusband if his wife could earn as much as he, and seems to do more than his share of cooking and housework anyway. Dennis, a painter and decorator, works extremely long hours – sometimes an 18-hour day. He needs to do this to support his large family, and there was a hint that he also likes to get away from them. He has a long history of doing domestic chores – ever since his widowed mother had to take a paid job and Dennis had an evening meal ready for her when she got home. He, like Frank, would willingly stay at home, if his wife could earn as much as he and was willing to get a paid job. Neither Frank's nor Dennis's wife have a particular skill, and could only work for a low wage. Darren, recently married building labourer, has a working wife. He anticipates that when they start having children, mainly for financial reasons, his wife will stay at home to look after them.

The unemployed young men, all of them unskilled and semi-skilled labourers, were almost unanimous in saying that there were no jobs which could be done by one sex only. They regard women as capable of doing heavy work though women might take longer, but they 'should be given a chance.' Richard (19, unemployed, single) stressed individual differences:

> Women can do everything now that men have always done. It depends on how a girl thinks of herself. She could do it physically and mentally, but if she did not want to get dirty she could not be a coalminer or a refuse collector. Differences are individual. I would always choose someone who could do the job.

Dick (19, unemployed, single) had 'come across a lot of women mechanics. A woman could be a panel beater, now that we have the technology.' He had seen 'many girls emerging from under a lorry or a jeep at pop festivals . . . they are as good as men at repairs'. An older man, Clifford (64, clerk, single) has

> never noticed that men and women were particularly good at any job because of their sex. It is often said that they are, but I would not regard it as a good enough reason for any particular job being done by a person of one sex, rather than another.

Many men felt that although men and women could be equally good or equally inefficient, the general public has very different expectations. Ranjeev (26, cohabiting) found this during his nursing career:

> Being a male nurse you are either liked because you are a guy, or you are disliked . . . it is seen as a 'female' profession and you are different. There is a high expectation of male nurses. Supposedly they are more gentle, but if they are not quite up to scratch they are considered useless, so it works both ways. As a midwife I came across only two mothers who objected to a male midwife. Others made no distinction, it is the person that matters.

Vince (30, cohabiting) also a nurse, found that patients treated male and female nurses alike, and his own view is that sex makes no difference to how good a nurse is at his/her job. However, he noticed that female nurses on casualty tended to steer female patients away from male nurses. While he worked as a midwife, all mothers and their partners were asked if they had any objection to a man, and remembers only two who did. It was female colleagues who emphasised the difference.

> Female nurses used to say that male nurses could get away with more things . . . if anything, we had to work harder to prove yourself, to make your presence felt, make an impression. There is nothing a woman cannot do. Some girls I know work in coal mines, they can become firemen.

A number of men who were not sure if women could do every job that requires physical strength were strongly in favour of not denying them the opportunity of proving they could do it. 'I am not certain about manual labour, but women should be given the chance. It remains to be seen if they can do it' (Hugh, 37, lecturer, single). Sanjay (32, taxi driver, married) expressed the same sentiments:

> Men and women can do the same work, my mother was a doctor. Women have not been given the opportunity to do the same jobs as men, so we cannot say. I have never seen a woman driving a crane, or building a wall. I am sure she could, given the chance.

Gerald's wife was for a time a manager of a residential establishment. He was surprised at the reaction of his social work colleagues when she got the job. They were amazed by the fact that the post had not been filled by a man.

Many men expressed the view that both men and women should be allowed and encouraged to get to the top, but many recognised that there were many more obstacles of a varied nature preventing women from not only reaching the top but working at all. Ranjeev (previously quoted) pointed out that 'there are not enough facilities such as creches and paternity leave'. To succeed, it was recognised that sometimes women have to be tough, 'have a steel quality'. Stanley (23, money broker, single) describes his girlfriend, a successful estate agent, as 'soft on the inside and tough on the outside'.

There was disagreement whether men or women made better bosses and whether gender entered into it at all. Some views seemed to be coloured by personal experiences. Ramah (19, unemployed, single), for instance, considers 'female bosses more helpful and understanding', while Trevor refers to female managers as 'super-efficient' and 'hard'. On reflection, he thought they had to be like this to succeed. Clifford (previously quoted) related in detail an experience he had at work of not consulting a woman who thought she was in charge. Although she was unpleasant and 'made a fuss' Clifford has not allowed this episode to influence his judgement, and generally thinks men and women are capable of holding top positions.

A few men expressed the belief that men get on better than females with others at work, for instance Lionel (55, draughtsman, single):

> Women fall out with people they work with, go on without speaking to each other . . . have more problems handling other people, men resent working under them. Women explode and find it hard to get back on an even footing, but if a woman wants to work or open her own business, I say good luck to her.

John (30s, photographer, married) expressed some hope for the future:

> There are more and more women doing manual work. It is becoming obvious that women can succeed in what were traditionally the manual workers' jobs. I don't know how many women work in the mines, but the number will increase. If there are occupations where there are not many women it is because of prejudice and this will change.

On the subject of equal pay, with one exception all the men pronounced themselves in favour, though for different reasons. It was recognised that it would be difficult to define work of equal value, and this leaves many loopholes and opportunities for evasion of treating men and women equally. The concept of equality was, by some, thought to have little value without incorporating equal access to better-paid jobs. These were some of the reasons given to support 'equal pay': 'the husband may be out of work and the wife may have to support the family' (Craig, previously quoted). Benjamin (37, clerk, divorced, single parent) thought everyone should be equally able to support themselves and their families, both men and women could find themselves in that position. Jacob believes that there should be a proper rate for the job, and lower pay for women would mean lower pay for all. All those in their 80s tended to see this as the main reason for financial equality. Their reasoning was pragmatic, rather than based on a principle.

Of those two who believe in differential pay, one justified it by the social expectation that men should support their family, the notion of a family wage. A totally different reason was produced by Alex (54, scientist, divorced):

> Often, men and women are not doing the same type of work. A man is usually given more responsibility and if the task is accomplished he gets the credit. If not, he will bear the brunt

of any unpleasantness. He is called upon to play the tune, it is only fair that the piper gets paid more . . . In what is nominally the same job, the man will suffer more, will be reprimanded by his boss. He should be paid more in recognition of this. He will be pulled backwards through the hedge. I would hazard a guess that a female boss would be harder on him than a male boss.

As has been pointed out by others, the female boss may have struggled harder and longer to get to the top, and acquired her 'steel quality' on the way. Men like Roland, a personnel officer, have struggled hard to introduce equal pay and are very aware that the task has not yet been achieved.

A few men felt that in some situations men are now being discriminated against, and quoted examples of men and women applying for the same job and the woman getting it, even if less well qualified. The reason for this was thought to be that a man, if turned down, would not ask any questions whereas women would, as they are now protected by law. These men said they wanted to see justice done and the best person for the job should get it.

6
Relationships

Social relationships cover a wide range of interactions ranging from brief and casual encounters at social functions or on holiday to non-intense exchanges with neighbours, friendships of various degrees of closeness and marriage and cohabitation which, unless interrupted by death or divorce, can last between 40 and 50 years and which is all-embracing, being an economic and legal contract as well as a vehicle for sexual and emotional fulfilment. In addition to marriage and heterosexual cohabitation, many transient and lasting unions are formed between people of the same sex. For the purpose of this study only friendship, courtship and marriage were selected, 'marriage' including stable cohabitation between people of the opposite or same sex. Within these relationships only certain aspects were selected – as indicated in the questionnaire. Housework, finance and decision-making within marriage are dealt with separately in Chapter 7, since I regard these as most closely linked to and reflecting the power structure within marriage and inequalities within it.

Friendships are an important source of happiness and pleasure for both men and women. Michael Argyle, a psychologist, on questioning a number of people, found that cementing a new friendship and being with friends is a major source of satisfaction, while losing a friend is a very stressful event. In friendships there are no formal rules, but many informal ones such as loyalty. When these are not observed the relationship is not likely to last. All friendships have common characteristics, in spite of cultural, class and gender differences, and Argyle and Henderson[2] sum these up:

Friends are people who are liked, whose company is enjoyed,

who share interests and activities, who are helpful and understanding, who can be trusted, with whom one feels comfortable and who will be emotionally supportive.

It is often asserted that gender plays an important role in both the quantity and quality of friendships. Argyle and Henderson sum up the qualitative difference: 'for men, friends are people to do things with, for example, shared leisure, while for women, friends are people to confide in, who will be emotionally supportive'. Women are believed not only to form more intense friendships, but also to have more friends. Men, particularly those middle-aged and working, often have few friends or none: instead they have mates, colleagues, customers and clients. Some of the main gender differences which have been found are that female friendships are characterised by more self-disclosures, intimacy, affection, social support and more talking than male friendships. Men, in cross-gender friendships, have fewer rules about touching or having sex. Women prefer to draw a line between friendship and close physical contact with a male friend. Men derive slightly less satisfaction than women from being together with friends. Men are more likely to meet their friends in places other than home: in clubs and pubs, or while playing sports.

It seems that social taboos on male expression of feelings and the value placed on male independence act as obstacles and deterrents to men being able to form close, confiding friendships, and that men need to justify being together by activities. Homophobia (fear of homosexuality) may, on an unconscious level, act as another barrier to intimacy between men. Because of socialisation men and women observe a different set of rules.

The existence of friendships, their formation and dissolution, seems to be based on 'the rewards' that friendships bring after 'counting' and deducting 'the cost'. Social exchange theory is one of the most plausible explanations.[16,48]. However, friendships cannot be considered in isolation from the social context in which we live. A man who sees himself as the breadwinner, and who regards his wife as a homemaker, may allocate little time to enjoying the company of those whom he would choose, rather than those with whom he shares his working environment. While marriage is regarded as potentially the main source of companionship and moral support, women who are isolated at home with young children, not working, and do not have a partner who is a good confidant, become depressed.[17] The high value placed on marriage can act as an obstacle to seeking satisfaction in close friendships and the existence of such does not altogether cushion the impact of divorce.[108]

The men in this book were generally agreed that both sexes have an equal need for friendship. A few men insisted that their own friendships with other men and with women were in no way different from the female friendships they had observed. The majority commented that men, as friends, behaved differently from women. Different reasons were put forward for the disparities. Some men regretted that pure male/female friendships were sometimes not possible because of outdated social convention, and quite a number expressed a preference for having female, rather than male, friends.

The need for friends was stressed by men of all ages and in different occupations. Craig (17, catering assistant, single) confided: 'I know a lot of blokes and a lot of girls, you are lost without friends.' While his mother has many friends he regrets that his father has too few. His parents were recently divorced and both need supportive networks. Dennis also stressed the need for companionship, but the difference between him and his wife is that her friends are mostly neighbours, his are his customers with whom he chats while decorating their houses, whenever he gets the chance. Charlie, aged 90 and widowed, bitterly regrets that all his friends are dead, and that the other men in the residential home where he lives are no longer mentally alert and he cannot talk to them. He has not tried to become too friendly with any of the ladies.

In the course of my interviews a long list of differences between how men and women treat their friends emerged. One of them was greater male competitiveness. 'Men are always trying to prove themselves, that they are better. Men like a fast car to show off . . . I suppose women like to show off too, but different things, their clothes, their boyfriends' (Craig). 'Showing off' is strongly disapproved of by Richard, who has adopted a totally non-competitive lifestyle and mixes with friends of both sexes (Richard, 19, unemployed, single). Ralph (50s, teacher, divorced) pointed out that 'men tend to meet other men in competitive situations such as playing football or cricket'. Alf (89, retired commercial traveller, widowed) reminisced that

> when men get together they always try to show off. They put each other down and they put women down, try to prove

they are more clever than their friends. It is all a bit of a game, it is just showing off in front of each other.

The belief that female friendships are longer-lasting and can withstand short-term and long-term separations found strong support. Stanley (23, money dealer, single) likes to keep in touch with his friends even though he has a girlfriend whom he sees regularly, while she prefers to spend all her time with him and has put her female friends in cold storage. 'She knows that she can keep in touch by 'phone or only see them very occasionally and they will understand and still be there.'

> Women can have close, long lasting friendships with other women much more easily than men do. I put this down to solidarity among sisters. I am not sure what men do when things are not going well. I have formed close friendships with other men, but they just stopped for no apparent reason. I regret this. (Hugh, 37, lecturer, single.)

Trevor (61, retired bank manager, married) believes the reason men do not keep in touch over long periods is that 'men are more self-contained . . . more concerned with material things, they talk about their jobs, getting on, men care less about friends'.

The belief that men talk less among themselves than women, and also about different things, underlines the comments made by Alex (54, scientist, divorced):

> Men recognise each other's qualities, women work harder at friendships. Men talk about fundamental things: politics, sport, education of their kids. Women talk more, but about more trivial issues.

This statement contains an inherent value judgement. Alf (previously quoted) believes that female friendships are an extension of general female interest in people and relationships:

> A man might speak to two or three people in the course of a day. A woman goes down the street and can speak to five female friends in the first five minutes. A woman wants to visit her neighbour and find out what Mrs So-and-so has been doing and if she has not found out, her visit would not have been worthwhile. Women like to find out things and it is in the woman's nature, a woman has got more time.

Relationships

The (mistaken in my view) belief that women have more time for friends was subscribed to by many men, especially those who work long hours or do heavy manual work. They see their wives and other women, even if employed outside the home, as having a great deal of time to spare. Activities that are seen as fit pursuits for a woman, such as shopping, are also seen as providing women with more opportunities to meet friends than men have. 'When you see women shopping, they usually stop to chat. All that men have time to say is "hello mate, all right?" Generally speaking, women are generally speaking' (Bert, 87, retired fireman, widowed). He would have liked to have made friends with his female fellow residents but alas, 'they are in a bad state'.

Many men regretted that whilst they had a number of friends at school and during adolescence, they have lost touch with them. 'I have no men friends', said Sydney sadly, but he does have a few female friends.

Quite a few men expressed a preference for female friends, who are considered more supportive, open about themselves, understanding, prepared to discuss a wider range of subjects. Barry (20, unemployed, single) prefers female friends because 'boys talk about boring things: cars, drugs and football. Women keep their friends for many years and keep in touch more regularly'. Donald (73, actor, divorced) has always liked women.

> I find them more complex. I find men easier to understand, maybe because I am a man. I prefer being in female company. Women are less predictable. Men tend to talk about what they are going to do, women are more concerned about other people, also what others say and think about them.

Donald went on to say that he thought men, rather than women, find it easier to make friends, working in mainly male environments and having interests that are easily shared, such as sport. As an actor he himself has worked with men and women. Having similar interests was seen as an important basis for friendships: 'I don't know what women do or say to each other, but I don't think they differ from men. People will seek out each other with similar interests, irrespective of whether they are male or female' (Troy, 58, retired scientist, divorced).

Regret was expressed about the fact that men and women could not always easily be just good friends with the opposite sex, although the younger men thought this was possible. Christopher (29, banker, single) noticed that, even in the last few years, things have changed.

> When I stopped living with my girlfriend a few years ago, it was as though I came back to a whole new world. Whereas boys used to go round in a crowd and girls in pairs either with a female friend or a boyfriend, now it is more acceptable to have a woman friend, just a friend with whom you would not have any physical involvement.

Simon (21, unemployed, single) would like to keep in touch with some of his ex-girlfriends whom he genuinely likes, but warns of the hazards involved: 'just as you walk into a pub a bloke might hit you because he thinks you are after his girlfriend'. Ranjeev (26, nurse, cohabiting) has both male and female friends and urges caution with regard to what is talked about. 'One should make it clear that when one talks about sex generally, it does not always imply that one wants to have it with the person with whom one is talking.' There was a general feeling that friendships should be able to flourish and survive without any sexual involvement.
The male defence against disclosure of feelings and vulnerability is one barrier, aggression another, against closeness.

> Men make more superficial friends than they can handle, as you get older you lose some . . . a woman can count hers on her fingers and keep them longer. It is to do with nature, because women are not aggressive, do not put up their fists in the air. Some of my friends come on really strong and then a man has to defend himself. (Leroy, 23, unemployed, single)

A longing for closeness was expressed well by Clifford: 'I often feel jealous of the kind of friendships women have with each other. Men also need close relationships. Being a man can act as a barrier.'
Courtship in former times, according to historians[32,99,101] was characterised by community and kinship participation and ritual. Courting and dating were organised by kinship groups and meetings took place in a public arena: at dances and festivals where groups of boys met groups of girls. A courting couple returning home after dark was usually greeted by their village

neighbours and barking dogs. A girl's and her parents' choice of a suitor was indicated in the prescribed manner, such as picking up his ribbon at a dance and a special arrangement of logs on the fire.[99]

In England and many parts of Europe in the seventeenth, eighteenth and early nineteenth centuries the practice of bundling was widespread. The courting couple were allowed to lie together all night, the degree of undress and the parts of each other's body they were allowed to touch being strictly prescribed.

Collective dating gradually gave way to a more individualistic style, and the idea of romantic love legitimised individual choice. Even today, however, in some countries such as Greece, Spain and parts of Italy, courtship is supervised and girls chaperoned.[62] The idea that the man woos the woman, and she accepts or rejects, has not died out, even in our society. 'Attractive females are not more competent than other females: they do not need to be, since men take the initiative.'[2] This statement is not borne out by the men in this book. Initiating relationships, and who should pay for entertainment on a date, were singled out for special attention on the assumption that these two areas are strongly affected by stereotypes: the bill in a restaurant is invariably placed before the man.

The idea that men rather than women should initiate intimate relationships found very few supporters. The overwhelming majority of men seemed convinced that both sexes should feel equally free to make the first move. Some men described how they felt when approached by women, and many regretted that some women still hold traditional views and leave the initiative to the male. It was felt that men also need to change. Clifford (64, clerk, single) warns us against the dangers of generalisation:

> It is difficult to say who really initiates a relationship. Some women or men may do it in a very subtle way. Some women may not want to take the first step. I am very weary of generalisations. Some men might be put out if a woman approached them. That would not apply in my own case.

Trevor (61, retired bank manager, married), on the other hand, feels not only that men should take the initiative, but also that 'women like men to initiate relationships. A man who was approached by a woman might feel flattered but also think of himself less as a man.' Similar sentiments are expressed by Alex (54, scientist, divorced):

Relationships

A man expects it of himself and a woman expects it of a man to be the prime mover. This is what I would expect of myself. If a woman approached me, it would be a pleasant surprise provided I liked the woman.

Equality was seen as an ideal by most men. 'It is rubbish that it is up to the bloke to make the first moves' (Richard, 19, unemployed, single). Eamonn (59, social worker, divorced) believes that 'the days of the hunter and the hunted are long gone. It should not be left to the man to chase women. She can also start the whole thing going.' 'Some men and women are equally shy. Traditionally men are expected to take the initiative, but there is no logic in it. Although many men may not like to admit it, often women do initiate relationships' (Bob, 65, probation officer, single). Alf (89, retired commercial traveller, widowed) has changed his views over time, 'you get a shy man and a shy woman, whoever is less shy should speak first'. Craig thinks that if girls and boys do not feel free to take the first step

> a silly situation may result with a boy in one corner and a girl in the other, both equally shy and neither making a move. Although some men may feel a bit dented by being asked out by a girl, they should not do so. (Craig, 17, catering assistant, single)

A few men freely admitted to not ever wanting to make the original approach. 'I have never made the first move, never had enough guts to do it' (Murray, student, cohabiting). Simon (26, unemployed, single) believes that 'it should be whoever has had a few drinks and gets bored sitting alone first'.

Some of those men who had been asked out by women at first felt surprised, but all were overall pleased and flattered. Chris (29, banker, single) described the following scenario: 'There was a girl in a pub and she started chatting me up. I found it quite amusing at first, but if she is attracted to someone, why should she not show it?'

More freedom was advocated by many. 'It would be nice if girls felt free to ask a man to go with them more often. It is still the man who usually does it. I would not feel embarrassed if a girl asked me out; some men might' (Ramah, 19, unemployed, single). Leroy (23, unemployed, single) has strong views on the subject:

> More women should come forward so that we become equal. Too many men come forward and some girls are very insulted by this. When I see a girl at a disco, I think why don't she come forward, because she is standing there, waiting to be asked and this is irritating me. I wonder if my asking would insult her, but a man should also be rational and not afraid to ask.

Donald (73, actor, divorced) feels that 'things need to progress, women have been conditioned to wait, it is time that the barrier was pulled down'. But according to Troy (58, retired scientist, single) this will not happen overnight. 'Many people feel it is up to the bloke to make all the running, you cannot expect any social change to take place quickly. I would be absolutely delighted. I wish somebody would ask me out occasionally.' Sanjay (32, taxi driver, married) hopes that social encounters can shed their sexual connotations.

> Because of the past, we tend to think that if a woman invites us out she wants to go to bed. It has been drummed into us that if a woman makes a go for you, she wants sex. It would be nice if this was eliminated, if she can invite you out and start a friendship. It would be nice if we got to that stage.

The views of the study men on financial arrangements when a couple go out together were, in spirit, similar to the views expressed on initiating relationships: most men favoured equality and most were fairly pragmatic taking into account the practicalities. These considerations included who happened to be working or have more money. There seemed to be little recognition of the symbolic meaning of money and that it could represent power as well as being a way of 'spoiling' someone.

Those who thought that the man should foot the bill spanned all age groups. It was not just the oldest men and one of them, Alf, has what he described as 'modern ideas'. Jacob (78, retired butcher, widowed) believes, as he always has done, that 'a man should pay and the lady accept gracefully and if she won't, he should take someone else out'. Jimmy (28, unemployed, single), a representative of the younger generation, shares Jacob's views: 'The man should pay, I suppose it's only right . . . I have no reason for saying so.' Jonathan (17, unemployed, single) gave his reasons: 'it looks better if the man pays. I would want to pay to spoil and impress my girlfriend, men do that sort of thing.' Alf (89, retired commercial traveller, widowed) used to pay when he took his fiancée for a treat.

> If a woman knows that the man cannot afford to pay, she can offer and he should accept gracefully. It is nice for a man to openly make a fuss of a woman and not be ashamed of it. You should do gentlemanly things like opening doors for either a man or a woman, if he or she is carrying a heavy bag.

Some men, specially young ones with little money, said they liked to spoil their girlfriend and spend whatever money they had on her, but would do so equally with a male friend they liked. Barry, unemployed, likes to take his girlfriend for special treats to show her how fond he is of her. If ever there is any money left over he likes to buy drinks for his male friends, or flowers for his landlady, in lieu of rent. He feels it is very wrong to use money to 'show off'. Leroy (23, unemployed, single) also likes to spend money while he has it, to show the extent of his caring. 'I will spend my money until I am broke and then ask her [girlfriend] to pay. When S. . . was skint, she asked me for money and we both felt really good about it.'

Many men were quite uncertain what they felt and liked to do. Eamonn (59, social worker, divorced) was among them. This is how he portrayed his dilemma:

> I tend to be a little bit old-fashioned. It is the way I have been brought up. I like to put a woman on a pedestal. I will also go along with 'going Dutch'.

For some men the circumstances were important – whether it was the first date and a public or more private place. Clifford (64, clerk, single) suggested that because of social convention

> if it is the first date, it should be the man, but this is only social conditioning. With equal pay, in proper relationships, people should share the expense. A great deal would depend on the personalities of the people involved.

Karmi (48, lecturer, divorced) believes that 'whoever issues the invitation should pay, unless it was mutually agreed to share the cost'. Ramah (19, unemployed, single) made a distinction between being in a public and a private place.

> If I was in a restaurant with a girl and she had to pay the bill, I would feel a bit embarrassed. I think we should go 50/50 but she should give the money to me. I would not mind her paying say for a taxi, when no-one can see.

He did admit that on the occasions when he did not have much money he agreed to women paying the restaurant bill.

Those who believed in equal shares suggested a variety of arrangements such as taking turns at treating each other. Ralph (50s, teacher, divorced) thought it should be 'from each according to his ability to each according to his need'. He assured me that this also included 'her'.

A few men were critical of women they had been out with and who expected to be paid for. 'A woman should pay her share. Some women want the best of both worlds and to be paid for' (Ivor, 65, retired clerk, divorced). Bob (65, probation officer, single) also complained 'some women expect the man to pay. Those are the ones I do not particularly favour. I like those who pay their way. Most women dive quite naturally into their bag.' Lionel (55, draughtsman, single) claims to have come across some women who have tried to take advantage of him. 'Some women are very greedy, a man usually sets a limit on how much he is prepared to spend, depending on how much he likes the woman.' Karmi despises men who pay for women and expect them to repay by looking glamorous. Although brought up in a culture in which women were expected to please men, his ideas are totally different. Craig (17, catering assistant, single) equally disapproved of men who 'show off'. 'Some boys like to flash their wallet, get out the money, the man thinks himself bigger than the girl, "You owe me a favour", but it is much better if maybe I pay one night and she pays another. I do her a favour and she does me one.'

Marriage in contemporary Britain is a very popular institution, with 90 per cent of the population eventually getting married but not necessarily staying married, or not staying married to the same person. There are no precise figures for stable cohabitation or homosexual unions. In 1984, 396,000 couples got married in the UK, with 35 per cent being remarriages for one or both. In the same year, 158,000 got divorced.[21]

Modern marriage incorporates many strands and traditions,

including Christianity with its emphasis on permanency, fidelity and procreation. Historians have traced a progression, though uneven and not unilinear, from the sixteenth-century marriage based on total male dominance, lack of privacy, emphasis on the financial nature of the transaction to companionate marriage based on individualism, the ideal of personal happiness, and sexual fulfilment. The end result is a marriage which is 'a high-risk enterprise'[50] and which is based on 'serial monogamy'.[99] While some historians and sociologists emphasise the symmetrical nature of the couple relationship[113] and its complementary and positive contribution to happiness and socialisation,[88] others have drawn attention to the basic inequalities within marriage.[59,76] Feminist writers, especially, have pointed out areas of conflict in marriage related to gender inequalities.

The only respectable and freely admitted motives for being together are now love and affection, as well as raising a family. Other reasons of a more economic nature, such as acquiring a housekeeper or climbing up the social ladder by marrying into a higher social class, are not usually mentioned. Although mate selection is ostensibly based on free choice, the principle of homogamy operates. People with similar social characteristics choose each other.[24]

The question about what men and women expect from close relationships which include sex, and whether the sexes behave differently, received a variety of answers with as many men stressing the differences as similarities. There was no consensus and the only common denominator was that, with one exception, all the employed manual workers emphasised that in marriage their wives looked out for security and expected to be provided for financially, while men looked for love and sex. Only one, Frank, a self-employed builder, disagreed and thought that his wife expected more from life than that. The labourers saw themselves as living up to their wives' expectations and being good providers. Mike, who is married and has two young children, gave a detailed account of how his wife puts on her make-up, a nice nightdress and generally makes herself attractive 'to get round me when she wants something'. After an initial show of resistance, and claiming he is too tired for sex, Mike usually succumbs and a new outfit for her may be acquired on the Saturday morning shopping expedition.

While some men believe that it is women who need stability and security, Keith (31, banker, single) thinks it is the other way round.

Relationships

Men are more concerned with stability, funnily enough. A lot of men like to know what the rules are and to live by these rules, to make sure the rules are obeyed. They may be hypocritical rules and men may have a different set of rules to women. Women are not very good observers of rules. I have never met any girls who want stability. You only see girls who want blokes to propose to them on TV. Some men believe that if they can have more than one girlfriend and fool around a bit, it's OK as long as the girlfriend does not know about it. Women do not subscribe to this.

Keith admitted that when he was in his early 20s he 'might have been amused by this sort of thing' but he is now looking for stability. Jimmy (28, unemployed, single) believes that 'a woman, once she marries, wants to stay at home and looks for love and security. A man could never be happy staying at home and not going out to work.' John (30s, photographer, married) believes that, allowing for individual differences, 'men want the more immediate results sexually and emotionally, they look for immediate rewards, women see relationships in terms of emotional interaction, though immediate rewards are not unimportant'. The idea of men being more preoccupied with the physical side of relationships was also voiced by Daniel (37, vicar, married):

> Men have a greater interest in the physical side. It is more important to men than to women. Stability and emotional fulfilment are more important to women, but it is just a question of emphasis. It might have some basis in nature. It would make sense for the childbearer to seek stability and the progenitor to scatter his seeds as widely as possible. In terms of evolution it makes sense but I will stand corrected. All this is reinforced by expectations.

Jacob (78, retired butcher, widowed) considers that 'men, unlike women, are too preoccupied with sex'. Sanjay (32, taxi driver, married) also believes that males and females have a different approach to sex:

> Women have feelings in sexual relationships. Men can go with just anybody. A woman has at least to like somebody, not necessarily love them. She cannot just go off with a

stranger. We are talking about the normal, the average woman; some women could.

The notion that men are more romantic was shared by quite a few men. Donald (73, actor, divorced) subscribes to this view: 'Boys are more romantic, girls more emotional.' Troy (58, retired scientist, divorced) believes that men are not necessarily more romantic by nature but

> Women tend to expect men to be romantic, give them flowers. Because of this, women suffer more disappointments than men. Women think romantically, men do romantic things. Guys do what women expect them to do, it gives them [men] pleasure, but it is not entirely spontaneous. Women are more committed in relationships, men hunt a bit more. Men can be more detached about this sort of thing.

Bert (87, retired fireman, widowed) described in great detail his own courtship and marriage to support the image of the romantic gentleman.

> I have had a very happy life. I married a Scottish lassie. I met her by the side of Loch Lomond. I looked at her and I knew she was the girl I would marry. This was in 1923.

So that they could become better acquainted, Bert got a job near his girlfriend, Nessy, and eventually she came to London. They got to know each other, became engaged and got married.

> On February 3rd each year, on our wedding anniversary, I used to take her to Scotland and on December 4th every year, the day she came to London from Scotland, I bought her a bunch of yellow tulips, her favourite flowers. We were married for forty-two years. After she died I could not stay on in the bungalow . . . I missed her too much.

Eamonn (59, social worker, divorced) stressed the influence of upbringing and religion, and the different expectations that he has of women he works with and those he lives with. The woman with whom he lived for many years was at first very dependent on him and then changed quite dramatically.

Relationships

> On her fortieth birthday she had a new hairstyle, changed her image, became a career woman; it worried me greatly. I had been in control, now I had to accept that she was on the level. Men like women who are dependent, women don't necessarily want to be. If a lady is tough and brighter than you are, she becomes a threat. Quiet, little women are easy to deal with, specially when you come from my [Irish] background.

Alf (89, retired commercial traveller, widowed) stressed individual differences:

> It is individual what people expect. One husband may want to go to the dogs or the pub, have his freedom. Another may want to stop at home. One woman might say 'I want you to stop at home' and another be quite happy for him to go. If she has been at home all day, she may want to go out, and he should ask her. Another woman may be quite happy to stop at home but she should not stop him from going out.

The last phrase was Alf's prescription for a happy marriage.

Of those who believe that the sexes do not differ in their expectations, love, security, faithfulness and children were listed as the hopes that people have when they enter into marriage or cohabitation. Leroy (23, unemployed, single) is now thinking of setting up house with his girlfriend:

> I now have a serious girlfriend. Before, it was only for a month or so. I am working out what I want. I don't want a marriage in church. I don't want to chain her up. I want a friend. A kid is more a symbol of marriage than a piece of paper. If we understand each other well enough we will have a kid. I look for intelligence and for us to correct each other's ways if they are wrong. She is expecting the same.

Vipul (50, care assistant, married) expects 'support and lifelong commitment'. Trevor, who has been married for over 30 years, said that both he and his wife hoped for 'security, companionship and children'. They wanted to bring up their children well, but 'not push them too hard.' They wanted contentment and something that they found hard to define: happiness. Their expectations have been fulfilled within fairly traditional roles, Trevor's wife returning to work when the children were grown up. Gerald and his wife have been married for nine years and their hopes have materialised within non-traditional roles, with one or both working and at times his wife in a higher position and earning more money than he.

Changing attitudes were described by some men. A number were pleased that male and female expectations are becoming similar or the same, but not all. Harold, who is separated, feels that one of the outcomes of greater equality has been that women have become punitive towards all men, including those with whom they have a sexual relationship. 'They give or withhold sex as a reward for an emotional relationship. It is not longer the 60s notion of sex for everybody. Men believe they need sex more than women and this gives women a lot of power.' Dick, aged 19, who has never been married, also believes that these days women want more freedom than men. 'Men want a home and a wife, kids . . . a woman wants a husband but she also wants to be free.' While some men saw women as investing and expecting more from relationships, and therefore being more vulnerable, some men saw themselves as the more vulnerable sex, especially when a relationship breaks up.

Until very recently, many people subscribed to a double moral standard for men and women. Some still do. Being 'quite a boy' and 'sowing wild oats' was considered acceptable male behaviour. A female behaving in a similar manner could only earn a bad reputation and an 'illegitimate' child before contraception became effective and available. Many single mothers were confined to mental institutions such as Bedlam. Women had to be chaste so that titles and property could be passed on to legitimate heirs and the family act as a basis for 'proper' social placement. Even today, the majority of female petitioners claim that their husband's behaviour was unreasonable as a ground for divorce, and top of the list for male petitioners as a ground is the wife's adultery and not being able to live with her thereafter. This seems to be an indication that either men and women behave differently in marriage or have different levels of tolerance for different types of behaviour.

A national survey[55] claims that the double standard has disappeared. In reply to a question about extramarital sex, 96 per cent answered in the same manner for both the husband and the wife. Strong disapproval was expressed by men and women: it was considered 'always wrong' by 58 per cent, 'mostly wrong' by 25 per cent and 'sometimes wrong' by 11 per cent, to have sex with someone other than one's spouse. The men in this study confirm the views of the national sample. Only a small minority approved of the double standard of morality. One of them was Tom, more fully referred to in the chapter on individual biographies. His justification was that women take affairs more seriously than men. Men consider extramarital involvement as trivial, and do not 'betray' the wife in the way that she would let down her male partner. A few men confessed to having indulged in having more than one sexual relationship at a time, but being older and wiser now would find it boring. Owen, in his early 20s and in the motor trade, did not wish to fully take part in this survey but volunteered his views on sex:

> The car trade is the 'lecherous trade'. Most of my mates have an address book like the yellow pages, with girls' 'phone numbers. We boast about this but do not expect the girls to behave like we do. It is mostly men in the trade and about ten per cent girls. You see them dolly birds chatting up a bloke and then he gets interested in the car. This happens at auctions. He thinks the girl goes with the car. You see them buxom blondes spread over the bonnet, but when you come to think of it, it's really nothing to do with the motor, but it attracts attention.

Very strong disapproval of a double standard was expressed in different words and phrases: 'When a bloke goes out with all the girls he is a "great bloke", when a girl does the same thing, she is called all the names under the sun and I don't think this is right, it should be absolutely equal' (Craig, 17, catering assistant, single). Hugh (37, lecturer, single) emphasised trust: 'If you cannot trust each other, you should not be together.' According to Sanjay (32, taxi driver, married) 'if a woman is called a slut, a man who sleeps around should also be called a slut'. Alf (89, retired commercial traveller, widowed) shared his conviction:

> What is good enough for a man is good enough for a woman. There should be no moral distinction between how a man lives and how a woman lives . . . I don't know how to express myself there . . . if they are living together or are married, there should be only one moral standard.

His contemporary, Bert (87, retired fireman, widowed), quoted the marriage vows that he and his wife took: 'it should be for richer, for poorer, in sickness and in health, till death us do part' as it did part him from his wife, whom he loved very much. Daniel (37, vicar, married) believes in the existence of a universal moral law, 'moral dictates are equal for all. I believe this not just as a Christian.' Leroy indicated that he would go as far as breaking up a friendship with a male friend who was 'two-timing' a girlfriend. Richard (19, unemployed, single) expressed how his ideas developed.

> I went through thinking different ways about it. I used to think that my girlfriend would never go out with anybody else and if she did, I would beat him up and then, I thought maybe it is all right, and this is what I think now. Both should go out with others if they want to.

Jimmy (28, unemployed, single) thinks that 'it is all right to have more than one boyfriend or girlfriend at a time, but I have never known anyone who did.' For Simon (27, unemployed, single) triangles do not work:

> Everything should be always agreed and talked about, we are conditioned to 'one man, one woman'. Maybe some triangles could work. In my case, it is often the other way round: my girlfriend has someone else and I hang on to her.

Simon feels that men can be more vulnerable than women as men can become more attached and dependent on their partner than the other way round.

Close relationships come to an end for a variety of reasons. A number of studies have concentrated on those that arise from individual pathology and interaction between the couple,[26,104] It is not possible to explain the ending of marriage or cohabitation without taking wider social factors into account, and this has also been done.[41] Divorce has been made easier by legislation ever since in 1857 it came under the umbrella of civil law. The 1969 Divorce Reform Act has attempted, if not succeeded, in eliminating the idea of 'matrimonial fault'. Since the Legal Aid and Advice Act 1949, divorce has become more available financially. Social factors which affect divorce rates include high expectations of marriage, isolation of the nuclear family from kin and community, the challenge presented by the demands for equality by women and possibly most significantly increased demand for female labour which has made it possible for women to be independent. Most divorce proceedings are initiated by women, seven out of ten divorce petitions being presented by wives.[21]

On the basis of research, it appears that when a close relationship breaks up men are even more vulnerable than women. Men are more shattered,[75] take longer to recover and reorganise their life, some do not manage to do it.[107] In the majority of cases (some 90 per cent) the children stay with their mother, and it has been estimated that a third of the non-custodial fathers lose touch immediately, and more as time goes on.[27,66,67]. Although bringing up a child as a single parent can be difficult, the parent who loses touch with his/her child – usually the father – can feel deeply hurt and unhappy[1] and is missed by the children.[75,106]

Although no specific question was asked about the ending of relationships, some men volunteered their views. Some of these had parted from their girlfriends, others have been through divorce. One of them, Simon, today believes that men are more vulnerable, women much more sensible. The child which his girlfriend had by him stayed with her and has been adopted. Another man, who fathered a child in his early 20s, only sees her very occasionally and also feels sad about this.

Two factors most frequently mentioned as leading to a breakdown of marriage were money and infidelity. Trevor, a retired bank manager, feels that today's society is far too materialistic. People are prepared to spend extravagant sums on things like eating out, they work too hard and do not have time to relax and enjoy each other's company. Vipul (50, care assistant, married) stressed the need some people have for more and more possessions. 'A couple may work so hard for a new three-piece suite that by the time they come home they have no time to sit on it and by next year their suite is out of fashion; they have no time for each other.' Bert, in his 80s, also feels that 'today, people only live for money'.

Infidelity was seen as the reason for break-up by Jacob (78, retired butcher, widowed):

> The reason that so many couples get divorced is that the husband is carrying on with other women and his wife finds out. The husband usually says 'I am sorry I will be late tonight dear, working', and he has a date with one of the

girls in the office. A lot of things go on with regards to sex and it is shocking.

Karmi, who is divorced, had a very egalitarian relationship with his wife, doing his share of the housework and more than his share of the child care. He feels that the reasons for his marriage breaking up were not within the relationship but a sign of the times. His wife, an executive, did not think that her image of a career woman could include marriage. She held a high-powered job and wanted to be free.

Harold, who is separated and has had quite a difficult time as a single parent, regrets that men do not seem to get as much support as women do in terms of practical help and sympathy when their marriage ends, from friends, relatives and social services. He feels that women support each other. It has also been shown that divorced women, particularly with children, do not get much support and are not as welcome at social functions as divorced men.[45,60,70] Men also have been found to have a difficult time.[39]

7
Housework, Decisions, Finance

Housework is rarely classified as 'work'. Official statistics deny it the same status as paid work and the general public describe those who do not earn a financial reward as 'not working'. Yet, as was so rightly pointed out by Graham (Chapter 10: Individual Biographies) an employee very often could not do his/her job unless serviced by a housewife, usually a woman. In the English language 'housewife' has no male equivalent. According to government figures, 28 per cent of married, and 9 per cent of single, women aged 16–60 are full time housewives.[21]

The image of the happy housewife, with plenty of free time which she shares drinking coffee with other similarly placed friends and neighbours, has been shattered by researchers who discovered and documented dissatisfaction and a high incidence of depression among housewives. In a classic study of housewives, Ann Oakley[82] found that 70 per cent of her informants were dissatisfied with their role, this being related to monotony, isolation and low status. Those who had previously had an interesting job, those unable to live up to their own standards of housework, and middle-class women, were particularly dissatisfied.

Housework has many components, and of the six items specified (ironing, washing-up, cleaning, washing, shopping and cooking) shopping and cooking were strongly preferred while ironing and washing-up were strongly disliked. The average weekly hours spent on housework were found to be 77. Some of the husbands were said to be helping, and various degrees of participation were reported. A quarter were described as 'highly participating'. Oakley came to the conclusion that 'there are a significant number of marriages in which a general air of egalitarianism does not extend into the area of husband's housework and child-rearing behaviour.[82]

Eleven years after the publication of Oakley's research findings, a national survey[112] came to a very similar conclusion in the 1980s. Housework, despite the growing numbers of women in paid employment, is almost exclusively done by women. The survey questions about housework were split into seven components: household shopping, preparation of evening meal, washing up dishes after the evening meal, household cleaning, washing and ironing, repairs of household equipment and organisation of household money and bills.

Single and married/cohabiting people were asked who should perform various tasks and who actually did. Certain tasks remain, according to the replies given, traditionally feminine: these are cleaning and laundry, whereas men seem more prepared to do shopping and washing-up. Household repairs were mostly done by men. There was a considerable discrepancy between men and women in their perception of who did what. However, there was agreement that housework is predominantly done by women (as reported by 87 per cent of married women and 75 per cent of married men). There was also a disparity between reality and what was considered ideal. More people believe in than practise an equal division of domestic work. Young, working, married women are particularly in favour of equal distribution of tasks and are also most heavily burdened by the dual pull of paid work and housework. The authors of the survey concluded:

> We found that the domestic division of labour is remarkably unequal. Women were found largely responsible for the day-to-day care of the maintenance of the home with men assuming major responsibilities only for repairs of household equipment.

My questions about housework included a number of items: shopping, cooking, washing-up, laundry, cleaning, gardening, car repairs, maintenance of equipment and entertaining. The men were asked who in their view should perform the various tasks, and those currently married/cohabiting and those who had been, were asked about their practice. It is in the area of housework that I found the greatest discrepancies between beliefs and their implementation, as well as a great deal of uncertainty and confusion. Whereas some men felt that men can excel at cooking, there was almost universal consensus that women are better at cleaning, and even in some of the most egalitarian of marriages, washing and ironing were left to women. It was interesting to glean how decisions about housework were arrived at. Mostly they were based on unwritten rules and assumptions which were not discussed, even though the same men stressed the value of properly negotiated agreements.

Only the five oldest men in the sample seemed to have totally clear-cut ideas and had abided by what they felt was right. They and their wives adhered to highly segregated roles within the household: each performed tasks which were assumed to be their responsibility with hardly any consultation with each other, but the tasks were always accomplished to their mutual satisfaction (according to the informants, the wives' version might have been different).

This was said by Alf (89, retired commercial traveller, widowed):

> A woman should run the home and family. The husband should help, if his work does not make him too tired, but if he comes home tired, he should be left alone to regain his strength. A wife should put her home and her family first, even if she is working.

Jacob's ideas were expressed thus:

> It is a woman's job to get the house cleaned up and do the cooking. Women are definitely better at housework. It is not the husband's job. He should go out to work and bring the money. I went out to work and my wife never did a stroke of work in all her life. (78, retired butcher, widowed)

Here, the idea that only work which is paid for merits that description is strongly embodied in Jacob's world-view. Bert, also widowed, described in great detail the idyllic life that he and his wife had together, her excellence at domestic skills and how Bert always came home to tea 'beautifully cooked'. They shared gardening while Bert did most of the painting and decorating.

Such a rigid division of roles was not only advocated and practised by the older men, but favoured by some young ones. Those who had never been married intend to put them into practice.

Nineteen-year-old Ramah does not want to marry in England and intends to return to Pakistan.

> Stuff like cooking and washing clothes, a woman should do all that, but a man should do car repairs, painting and decorating. Women are naturally better at housework. I would expect my wife to do things in the kitchen, while I did things around the house. Girls are used to cooking and washing, helping their mothers. I would be unhappy if my wife only wanted to do half.

Ramah was brought up within a very traditional family. Jimmy's (28, unemployed, single) mother and sister did everything 'because Dad was not a handyman'. In spite of his background, Jimmy believes in traditional roles. 'Normally a woman does all that [housework]. Sometimes the man should clean. A woman is much tidier by nature. Women can repair cars, but it is a man's job.' Sydney, who is divorced and lives alone, admitted that he cannot cook and lives mostly on tinned food and takeaways. If he decided to live with a woman 'she would have to do all that'.

A number of married men who believe housework should be done by women are firmly putting their ideas into practice. For instance Mike (30, labourer, married) claims 'I don't know one end of the hoover from the other'. His wife does all the housework and most of the gardening, while Mike 'would not let her touch the car and I do all the decorating and whatever needs doing to the house'. Darren, very recently married, expects his wife, who also has a paid job, to do the housework, while he looks after the car and the structure of the house. Both of them, with the help of friends, decorated and cleaned their house before moving in. Vipul, married, believes in 'helping' with the housework but that it is his wife's responsibility.

Some men, like Alex (54, scientist, divorced) adopted an intermediate position. While believing that there should be a division of tasks along traditional lines, they advocated that the man should teach his wife to do the things that he normally does, and vice-versa.

> There is no reason why a man should not participate [in housework], but he only has a certain amount of time and each should be deployed to the maximum good of the family. It would take a woman hours to repair the car. He should

> instruct the wife, get her to understand mechanical things in case he becomes ill. She should instruct him how to cook. A man should not be left untutored. Men are more used to, less afraid of, electrical appliances; women quicker at cooking. A woman can get a decent dish together in no time, it would take a man all day. Cleaning should be shared.

Some men stressed that the time available often dictates how domestic jobs are shared, and that individual skills and aptitudes should be taken into account. Dennis, a married painter and decorator, is a highly skilled cook, having had to learn when his father died and his mother had to earn a living. He would prefer to stay at home, cook, and look after the house, but his job does not allow him to do so. According to Harold (56, lecturer, separated) 'people should do what they are good at and what they do not mind doing. Jobs which no-one wants to do should be shared equally, all according to the time available.'

Karmi (48, lecturer, divorced) described how one of his previous girlfriends, who was tall and strong, did all the decorating while he made her cups of coffee. Another girlfriend was small and dainty and did not like decorating. It was she who provided tea and coffee while he put up the wallpaper and applied coats of paint. Keith (31, banker, single) prefers a liberal approach.

> It should be whoever wants to do it. If no-one, then someone should be paid to come in and do it. This would be so in my case. Women might be better at housework, simply because they had done it before. They are not by nature good at it, anyone who shows an aptitude for washing a dish is going to be better than me.

Some of the men who did not normally do a great deal of housework either because their wife 'had more time' or was 'better at it', in certain circumstances, believed it was their duty and did all of it very efficiently. While Eamonn's partner was ill for several months, Eamonn did everything including nursing her, having had professional nursing experience. Frank, a self-employed builder, while his wife was recovering from an operation, installed double-glazed windows in his daughter's room, helped his son decorate his house, kept the house clean and after coming home from work cooked supper for his four children, his wife and his daughter's boyfriend, who was staying with the family at the time. His wife's health is not good and he generally does a fair amount of housework.

Of those men who genuinely believe in sharing all the chores, some are very lucky; for instance Murray (23, student, cohabiting) who said 'I hate ironing and my girlfriend does it. I do all the cooking and she hates it.' Some of the others who believe in equal shares pointed out that there were some things that their wives were better at. For instance, Ranjeev, who lives with his girlfriend, said he has a 'psychological barrier to cooking' but his girlfriend is teaching him.

> I have always insisted on equality, otherwise there would have been hassles and superficiality. She (current girlfriend) does most of the cooking, but only because she likes it. I do breakfast and washing up. With my previous cohabitee we split everything, but I was less concerned with the dusting. We had different standards, men notice dust less. Women tend to be cleaner.

Hugh (37, lecturer, single) explained how he shared housework:

> We did everything in turns. She taught me how to do washing-up. Sometimes she had to remind me. She liked cleaning and every time we had an argument she would refuse to speak to me for a day or two and she would spring clean the house.

Simon (28, unemployed, single) pointed out a discrepancy between ideals and practice:

> Ideally, everything should be shared but there are certain areas where I don't do as much, e.g. to do with keeping things ideally clean. I am prepared to leave things. We have just bought a dishwasher and I load it up. My wife spends more time in the tidying role, I mend the car. We both spend time in the kitchen. We both go out to [paid] work.

Sanjay's wife works part-time, he drives a taxi. They tend to spend equal amounts of time on housework. Sanjay went on to say:

My wife does the washing, I don't know how to separate the clothes. I do most of the hoovering. My wife usually does the toilet and bathroom, I do it now and again, I do dusting, change beds, clean windows. She does the ironing. When she is in the kitchen I go in with her and usually do the less skilled jobs like salads, peeling vegetables and washing up. The way we do things, it just happened.

On the subject of cooking, Jeremy said that while he was married, most things were shared, but he always did the cooking, and Leroy (23, unemployed, single) put forward the idea that 'women were not born to be good cooks. My mother was a good cook, she passed it on to me. A lot of girls these days cannot cook. I may pass it on to my son but not to my daughter.'

Of all the tasks, entertaining was least often seen in traditional terms of the woman doing the cooking and the man dispensing alcohol. One of the suggestions made was that whoever is closer to the visiting friends or relatives should be free to talk to them most, and the other partner take on catering; another suggestion was that the person who issued the invitation should bear the main responsibility.

The need for a properly negotiated agreement was stressed by several men. Simon (27, unemployed, single) explained 'you cannot just split housework exactly down the middle, people should talk about it'. Bob (65, probation officer, single) thinks that by the time people are living together it may be too late for negotiations.

> They should work it out before living together. Women have had more practice at housework, but men can be good cooks. Nothing to stop men learning how to do everything if they really try. Both should welcome their guests and look after them. If a woman has a more steady hand, she should pour the drinks.

The process of negotiation is often a very subtle one, and arrangements are not discussed, but assumed on the basis of traditional allocation of tasks. Ralph (50s, teacher, divorced) who appears to have strong moral principles in a number of areas, such as advocating nuclear disarmament and equality in all spheres, did not succeed in doing it in his marriage, regarding housework.

We never actually discussed it. I always washed up. She cooked every night, she hated it. She was a very conventional person. She cooked out of a sense of duty, because she felt that this was the way society was ordered. Our first meal together she cooked and I washed up, and this is how we carried on. There was a certain assumption on my part that when I got home a meal would be waiting for me.

Ralph's ex-wife did freelance work mostly from home.

The discrepancy between hopes and aspirations and the reality of everyday living is described by Daniel (37, vicar, married):

When we got married our assumption was that we would play much more equal roles than we are doing but once we had a baby we imperceptibly slipped into the mode of my doing less housework. My wife works part time. Since she started working, the balance has been somewhat redressed. I cook the main meal twice a week, wash up and do some cleaning.

A few men complained that they were prevented from doing a fair share of housework. Benjamin (37, clerk, divorced) was one of them. While his wife was happy for him to look after the baby, she 'kept me out of the kitchen. It is not that she especially liked cooking, but she came from a very traditional [Irish] background and felt it was her duty.' Many men stressed that equality can only be achieved if both sexes accept it, if women are prepared to do their share of traditionally 'male' jobs around the house and let men do what are considered by some traditionally 'female' ones.

The process of decision-making has many levels and dimensions. Certain decisions are taken by individuals, others negotiated between the couple and some are to a large extent taken out of the hands of individuals and couples by existing social conditions and assumptions. This last level of social norms and economic structure is reflected, for instance, in the fact that it is usually the mother, not the father, who gives up work to look after the baby, the argument being not only that this is what nature intends us to do, but also that the father's earning capacity is greater than the mother's. While male employment carries higher reward and status, individual choices remain limited and, paradoxically, the unemployed may be in a more privileged position of being able to choose how child care is shared. More women than men choose where they live and work according to their husband's place of domicile and employment than the other way around.[112] Husbands are not usually prepared to follow their wives.

There has been little direct research on how important decisions are made. There is useful discussion on rules and metarules in the literature on the interior of the family and pathology.[4,57] The rules are obvious, metarules are at a more abstract, less visible level and determine who makes rules about what and the nature of the process. The functional school of sociology as represented by Parsons and Bales[88] considers that the family is divided vertically and horizontally by gender and generation. The parents are 'in charge' of rules for the whole family and each parent presides over a different sphere: the domestic and affectional sphere is the woman's province and the outside world the man's. The mother is the family's 'expressive' leader and takes decisions in this domain, while the father, being the provider and 'instrumental' leader, takes decisions related to this sphere. The notion of a proper 'parental coalition', a united parental front, has been seen as essential for familial happiness and mental health.[61] The trouble with this approach is that it does not take sufficient account of the unequal status of the adults within the family. It is very likely that the balance of power within marriage is based not only on feelings, but more importantly on who earns more and holds the purse strings.

The National Survey of British Social Attitudes in 1984[54] included two specific questions about decision-making. One related to the choice of living room colour scheme, the other to having children. The choice of the colour scheme was made mainly by the man in 5 per cent of couples and mainly by the woman in 48 per cent. The remaining couples chose jointly. The suggestion that the woman should decide how many children the couple should have found strong support from 27 per cent of informants, and 42 per cent disagreed.

Who makes the final decision to petition for divorce can be gleaned from official statistics;[21] twice as many wives as husbands set in motion the legal process which ends a marriage.

That the process of the decision-making is not as straightforward as it may appear was pointed out by Mike (30, labourer, married): 'My wife tells me what she wants, gets round me and then I pretend it's my decision.' In principle, Mike believes that the wage-earner, i.e. himself, should have the last word. Opinions were divided between those who firmly supported equality and those who insisted that the man should have the last word on most important matters. Pregnancy was seen as a matter for joint decision by as many men as those who believed that the woman should have the last word. Jimmy (28, unemployed, single) insisted that it is a male prerogative to have the final say in all things but 'the mother should choose the name of the child'. Ramah (19, unemployed, single) saw decision-making as 'the man's responsibility. A man should protect his wife. He should be responsible in that kind of relationship.' However, he excluded pregnancy from the orbit of male decisions: 'it is the woman who has to have the child'. Vipul (50, care assistant, married) advocated that 'the wife should be consulted'. He pointed out that 'many women who came to England from my country do not speak English and their husbands have to guide and protect them'. Jeremy (64, sculptor, divorced) invoked the natural law, 'a man would not be a proper man if he did not make some important decisions for both'.

This view was strongly opposed by Clifford (64, clerk, single) 'a man is no less a man if he does not make major decisions. If he did, it would suggest an artificial and strange relationship. Decisions must be based on sensitivity and understanding.' Joint decision-making was advocated in a variety of ways. 'Everything should be 50/50, including pregnancy. You should be hundred per cent sure, both of you, before you have a child. There are too many children in the world already. If both are to bring up the child, both must want it' (Richard, 19, unemployed, single). 'Both should be involved in decisions up to the neck' (Leroy, 23, unemployed, single).

Personalities and circumstances, it was said, should be taken into account. 'Decisions should be taken by whoever is more responsible' (Simon, 27, unemployed, single). He was not sure how the degrees of 'responsibility' should be assessed, but it was not along sex lines. John (30s, photographer, married) thought that 'decisions should be ideally joint, but the person who is at home may have more time to make the right kind of decisions'. In his case, both he and his wife are working. Graham (Chapter 10: Individual Biographies) believes that if the wife is at home she should make decisions on domestic matters and concerning the children.

Some men regretted that, although this is far from ideal, 'if they cannot agree, the man usually has the final say, he is physically stronger and shouts louder, but this is not right' (Craig, 17, catering assistant, single). Trevor (61, retired bank manager, married) thought it was more a question of personality than sex: 'whoever has the stronger personality gets their way'. Ranjeev (26, nurse, cohabitee) admitted to being 'the boss in all my relationships, maybe because my father was'.

External factors were emphasised by a number of men; these included work and earnings. Some men seemed to think that such decisions as who should stay at home, and where the family should live, were made outside themselves, by the society in which we live.

The decision whether to have children was seen by a number of men as the woman's prerogative. Such considerations as 'after all, she takes the physical risk' (Hugh, 37, lecturer, single) were thought important. 'I have seen too many girls damaged by unwanted pregnancy' said Barry (20, unemployed, single). According to Murray (23, student, cohabiting) 'a man's contribution to having a child is zero, compared to that of a woman. She should decide whether to have a baby.' Craig (already quoted) like Richard, believes that 'the couple should sort it out very carefully whether to have a child, unless there is one already on the way. Sometimes things just happen and then you are in trouble.' He related in detail the misfortunes of some friends of his who got married and had a baby in quick succession. The wife has had to give up her job after trying out five childminders.

All the men who have a view on decision-making felt that they had implemented it in practice, but not without their share of confusion, so clearly expressed by Ivor:

> There should be no necessity for a casting vote. It is nice when people think the same way. On the whole, the man should be dominant. It is wrong to say this but we have been trained to play dominant/submissive roles.

Lionel (55, draughtsman, single) finds justification for his uncertainty: 'Men should make decisions, having tried to get as much agreement as possible. How much a man gives in depends on the relationship. Women like it if a man makes the decision in some situations, but not always.

The question about finance was meant to elicit information about views and practice in three hypothetical situations: (1) only the husband, (2) only the wife, and (3) both earning money. A recent review of research and literature[56] on mechanisms of income distribution within the family refers to three main patterns among manual workers: firstly, allowance systems in which a proportion of the basic wage is allocated as an allowance for household expenses; secondly, whole wage systems under which the husband gives his wage packet to the wife and she gives back a sum for his pocket money; and thirdly, pooled earnings systems under which both spouses have equal access to any money earned and equal say in all decisions about money. There is some association between both spouses working and pooling their earnings. Young working couples were also found to operate the allowance system more frequently than pooling. The life cycle of the family has been found to be of relevance with 'pooling' of money being more common when both spouses are working and less common when the wife is at home, looking after children. Wives and husbands do not always have full knowledge of each other's earnings, and research conducted in the 1970s shows that this was so in 16 per cent of one sample[43] and 25 per cent of another[82].

In the great majority of cases where both spouses are earning, the husband's earnings are higher than the wife's. Not only are the average male earnings higher, but married women are more likely to work part time than their husbands or single women (Table 7.1).

Table 7.1: Relative earnings of husbands and wives when both working, UK, 1980 (percentages of couples)

Husband earns more	85.5
Wife earns more	9.0
Both equally	5.5
Total	100

Source: EOC, 1986.[30]

Equitable and just financial arrangements were seen by all men in the study as an important aspect of a stable relationship. Disagreements about money could lead to a break-up, and in some cases were seen as having contributed to it. The majority advocated an egalitarian arrangement and sharing of money, regardless of who earns it. Some men advocated that whoever was better at managing money should have the greater say. Retaining some small amount for personal needs/disposal was advocated by quite a number. All the men felt that they had put their ideas into practice, but a few of the divorced men regretted that they had not taken a tougher line and been less generous. Some wives were said to have concealed the amount of their earnings and regarded what they earned as 'theirs' and the husband's money as 'joint'. A small number of men emphasised they would want to retain major control over money.

All those in their late 70s, 80s and 90s said that whatever belongs to the husband belongs to the wife, and vice-versa. They never had any secrets from their wives and either 'put their wages on the table for joint use' or for those who had a bank account it was a joint one. Other younger and middle-aged men had similar ideas. Frank, in his 50s, a builder, has always shared his income with his wife, both having equal control. When Chris (29, banker, single) was living with a girlfriend, they 'always said it is ours. We gave money to each other. While I was earning more, I paid most of the bills, she paid for the shopping, we asked each other for money.' Trevor (61, retired bank manager, married) is a great believer in joint accounts: 'a joint account is far better than an allowance. In marriage, all money should be pooled.'

The majority of men who are or had been married have been in a situation where only they, but not their wife, were earning money. Others have or had wives who were in paid work, part- or full-time. A few had been unemployed while the female partner was earning. The majority thought that it did not make any difference whether both were earning and, if only one, whether it was the wife or the husband. The one who is at home was considered to be entitled to an equal share because 'either the wife or the husband should be able to stay at home. What each is producing is different. If one earns a salary, the other is entitled to it because his/her input is equal' (Benjamin, 37, clerk, divorced).

Murray (23, student, cohabiting) has been in three different situations: only he, only the girlfriend, and both earning money. 'Whoever earns more, should contribute more. The money was always shared equally between us.' Lionel (55, draughtsman, single) had a different view: 'If only one is working they do not have an equal entitlement. The wife should be entitled to a proportion, say 40 per cent. If the wife is working, but not the husband, he should rely on his savings for as long as they last.'

Lionel hoped that by the time the man's savings were exhausted he would have found a job, and did not relish the idea of financial dependency on a woman.

The idea of equality, but also having some money of one's own, to spend as one likes, was important to some men. For instance, Richard, unemployed, thought that each partner, if both were working, should keep some money for themselves, as well as contributing, according to earnings, to joint expenses. Hugh (37, lecturer, single) considers that 'the money belongs to both, whoever earns it, but it is good to have a little bit of independence and each have some money of their own.' Clifford (64, clerk, single) believes that:

> most money should be pooled but each should have a separate supply for small things. In a proper relationship, in which two people are equal, the idea of money belonging to one of them is very unsatisfactory and an old-fashioned concept. If an allowance is agreed on, it should only be for practical convenience, practicalities come into it.

One of the practicalities which was taken into consideration was who is better at managing money. Some men believe that sex does not come into it, some thought that women, others that men, were better. Leroy (23, unemployed, single) believes that women are better at looking after money – this has been his experience:

> I go out and buy this and that and have nothing to show for it. S. . ., my girlfriend, looks after my money. When I see men and women arguing about money, like my Mum and stepfather did, I cut off from it. It is chauvinist not to share money. It should be shared, it is what brought you together, the need to share.

Alf thought that some women, not his wife, are big spenders, and if a woman spends too much money on clothes or going to the hairdresser the husband should ensure that the children come first and there is enough money for essentials.

The need for proper negotiations and agreement was frequently stressed: 'the arrangement should be what the couple can genuinely agree on, but an agreement can be forced by all sorts of subtle pressures. The wage earner should not have more say, but unfortunately this often is the case' (Daniel, 37, vicar, married). Harold (56, lecturer, separated) thinks that a fairly formal arrangement might work best. 'The person who is doing housework should be entitled to an hourly rate. If I was doing it now I would say you are spending x hours working at home and it is worth so much. A 50/50 arrangement is not always fair.' Stanley, in his 20s, single, in principle believes that a 50/50 arrangement is only fair if both partners are doing either paid or unpaid work. If one chooses to stay at home, but does not do any housework and does not want to look after the children, s/he is not entitled to his/her share.

A few men admitted that they would want to retain a major say in how the money is spent, regardless of who earned it. Sydney (52, book-keeper, divorced) was unhappy with a joint account he and his wife had as he 'never knew where the money was going'. He described his wife as fairly irresponsible over money matters. Keith, a banker, would want to have a substantial say in major expenditure. He went on to say that, in his view, problems over money could only arise if money is in short supply, and this was not so in his case. Troy (53, retired scientist, divorced) included social convention among factors to be taken into account, while generally advocating equality:

> The earnings of both are part of joint assets. Ideally there should be a joint account, owned by both, but there are also accepted roles: the husband pays when the couple go out, women have coffee parties at home. Guys pop out to a pub for a pint. You cannot be too rigid. There are accepted norms and you have to observe them.

Troy went on to explain that both the husband and wife should have money for 'conventional' things or both go without.

Some of the pitfalls of a joint account were pointed out by a few of the divorced men: when a couple split up and no longer trust each other, working out fair shares can be a problem.

When asked if they had been able to put beliefs into practice, all the men said that they had done so, with the exception of those who felt that they had been exploited by their wives. Situations were quoted in which the husband's income was treated as joint, but the wife kept hers a secret and assumed it belonged to her. Such arrangements were seen as partly having contributed to the marriage not working. The bitterness generated before and during divorce might have also contributed to some men's feelings of injustice having been done.

8
Children

Throughout history, and even today, fathers and mothers have been presumed to be endowed with different qualities and have played different roles in relation to their children. It is not that fathers do not love their children and have not done so in former times. Although during the Middle Ages and sixteenth century, particularly, discipline was harsh and relationships remote, there are many historical accounts of the progress of 'affective individualism'[101] within the family from the seventeenth century onwards.

Mothers have always been expected to provide physical care, perform tasks which have brought them into intimate contact with their children and to be the source of unconditional love. The closeness of pregnancy has continued in different ways. The belief in instant mother love, and mothering instinct, have left many mothers feeling guilty and unhappy.[84] Father's stance, however, benevolent, has always been more remote and demanding.

The difference in social expectations and the behaviour of mothers and fathers has been documented by historians, e.g. Aries,[3] Flandrin[32] and Stone.[101] They have been portrayed by artists, justified by psychoanalysts and used as a framework for psychological research, as will be shown in this chapter. The father figure which emerges from this abundance of perspectives is someone who may have been quite indifferent to his children and preoccupied with their salvation while mortality rates were high; looked to them for support in old age; a patriarch whose authority has fluctuated; a rival for his wife's time and affection and currently a parent who may be present at the birth, plays with his children but is reluctant to change the nappy, supports the mother in her 'total maternal preoccupation' with the child[111] and helps her to regress and become dependent on the father, on the assumption that during the child-rearing stage the happiest families are dominated by fathers.[100]

It is only in the last few years that father–child interaction has been looked at in any detail, and those who have studied research findings comment on their sparsity.[93] Most of the research is American.[87] Only now is serious attention being paid to understanding parenting without preconceived ideas about gender roles, and old assumptions are being challenged, i.e. how much mothers actually enjoy the mundane aspects of child care.[82] Within the Women's Movement there are many different views about child care and how equality can be achieved, ranging from abolition of the family, advocated by Firestone[31] to plea for greater cooperation, by Friedan.[37]

Family historians offer fascinating insights into development of ideas about childhood and parenthood. Although there is disagreement about many issues such as the relative importance of economic change as a necessary precondition of changes within the family, there is a fair measure of agreement in many areas and similar descriptions of family life in former times can be found, based on personal documents, parish records, legal texts, paintings and iconography. It must be borne in mind that these documents are the work of literate men, thus the point of view and the experience of the poorer classes and of women has been filtered through the eyes of those able to contribute their perspective. Stone[101] refers to the principle of 'stratified diffusion': the norms and customs adopted by the rich and literate strata of the population become only slowly and gradually adopted by the less affluent and poorly educated people. It should also be remembered that various trends, such as lower mortality rates and moderation of patriarchal power of the father over his wife and children, have not been unilinear, and are subject to 'mysterious fluctuations'.[101]

One of the factors which is likely to influence parents' feelings for their children has been mortality rates. These did not begin to decline seriously until the middle of the eighteenth century, and before this around 75 per cent of children died in infancy. The likelihood of an early death was not conducive to a high emotional investment. Before the end of the sixteenth century births and deaths of children were often not even recorded, and it was common to give a newborn child the name of his deceased sibling. Enough children had to be conceived for some to survive and support poorer parents in their old age.

Children

Until the nineteenth century the interests of fathers and their children were often opposed. It was not possible for the mother to devote her time both to looking after young children and helping her husband in his business. Only breast-fed babies had a fair chance of survival, because of the hazards presented by polluted water and unhygienic conditions. At the same time, the performance by the wife of her 'conjugal duties' was likely to result in another pregnancy and drying up of the milk which, it was also believed, could be spoilt by sexual excitement. Many women, although condemned by the Church and the medical profession, had to resort to using a wet-nurse – usually a poorly paid woman who had little regard for the welfare of the infant. Flandrin[32] refers to wet-nursing as a 'murderous practice', resulting in a high death toll.

The eighteenth century was a time when the idea of childhood as a separate stage of life came into its own. Children's clothes, games and books made an appearance, and family portraits and paintings conveyed the new ideal of an affectionate, companionate family. The mode of address between parents and children became less formal, and there are accounts of close, loving relationships between fathers and children, e.g. the Boswell family.[101] At the same time, there are many descriptions in literature and legal documents portraying fathers as uncaring patriarchs anxious to exercise power over their children, invoking the natural law, regardless of the child's welfare. Such is a well-known account of the case of R. de Mannerville in 1804, when an eight-month-old child was forcibly removed by the father from its mother's arms, while feeding at her breast, and carried away almost naked in an open carriage in extremely cold weather.[67] Although the principle of the welfare of the child has dominated legislation since 1925 (Guardianship of Infants Act) it was not until 1973 that the Guardianship Act gave both parents equal rights as the guardians of their child.

Until the end of the nineteenth century it may be said that parents were more preoccupied with the survival of their children than child-rearing fashions and psychological theories. It was the father's right and duty, by virtue of the power delegated to him by God, to ensure that the child received a proper moral education and that his/her existence on earth, however short, was not sinful. It was the influence of Freud and his followers that focused attention on the legitimacy of enjoyment and pleasure in childhood. The psychoanalytic approach also emphasises the difference in the roles which the parents play in the child's development. The mother is seen as the parent to whom the child relates most closely and intimately during the first few months and years of life. Between the ages of three and five boys and girls are seen as wanting to be closer to the parent of the opposite sex, this having an unconscious sexual component. The 'Oedipal conflict' is resolved by identification with the parent of the same sex. Recently, it has been pointed out that because the parents play different, socially ascribed roles, a girl becomes like her mother, the parent she is close to and knows well, but who encourages her to care for the needs of others. A boy has to find his identity through becoming like a father, who is more remote and less available. He identifies with a stereotype of a father.[23] This often leads to inability to care for the dependency needs of others, and difficulty in openly acknowledging tender feelings.[47]

Nowhere is the idea of differentness between mother love and father love better expressed than by Erich Fromm in *The art of loving*[38] which deals with love in all its manifestations:

> The first months and years of the child are those where his closest attachment is to the mother. This attachment begins before the moment of birth, when mother and child are still one, although there are two. . . . The relationship to the father is quite different. Mother is the home we come from, she is nature, soil and ocean; father does not represent any such natural home. He has little connection with the child in the first years of life. But while father does not represent the natural world, he represents the other pole of human existence: the world of thought, of man made things, of law and order, of discipline, of travel and adventure. Fatherly love is conditional love.

Father's love has to be earned, mother's is given freely.

The idea that the bond between mother and child is special and different has led such prominent investigators as Dr John Bowlby to amass a great wealth of evidence from ethological studies of animal behaviour, and observation of children with their mothers. This has resulted in the formulation of attachment theory, according to which young children express a strong preference for being near a particular person, usually the mother, whose presence ensures their safety and survival. Bowlby suggested that deprivation of maternal care can have detrimental short- and long-term effects on mental health.[9,11-14] The heart-rending film made by Renee Spitz in 1945, 'Grief, a peril in infancy', portrays the suffering of infants separated from their mothers, as do the findings of Dorothy Burlingham and Anna Freud[18] during the Second World War. One may ask what effect did separation from fathers have. The work of Robertson,[95] and his film 'Two-year old goes to hospital', revolutionised hospital care of children. Most paediatric wards now have almost unlimited visiting hours and many provide accommodation for mothers, this having been advocated by the 'Platt Report'.[19]

Major studies of child-rearing practices have assumed and accepted that it is mainly mothers that care on a day-to-day basis for their children. One such example is the series of studies in Nottingham in the 1960s and 1970s, in which some 700 informants, all mothers, were asked about various aspects of bringing up children. The first study focused on infants,[78] the second on four-year-olds[79] and the third on seven-year-old children.[80] Although the questionnaire included questions about fathers, they were not interviewed. Another major study in the 1970s[113] also includes a question about fathers, but the underlining assumption is that fathers go out to work and 'help' their wives with child care.

It is paradoxical that the father–child relationship has been most carefully studied when the pair are no longer living under the same roof. A widely read textbook on issues in child psychology published in the mid-1970s includes a section on 'The importance of fathers'. Of the four chapters, three deal with absent fathers.[5] Children's reactions to divorce and absence of one parent (usually the father) have recently been well documented.[75,106,107]. Practical advice is offered to the non-custodial parent[96] and the advantages of continued post-divorce contact enumerated.[92] Some fathers are able to have a better relationship with their children after parental divorce than within marriage.[106]

What then is the reality of the current situation while the parents are married? Up-to-date surveys seem to come to very similar conclusions. May men and women believe that mothers of young children ought to stay at home and not go out to work. This view was supported by 60 per cent of women in a 1980 survey[71] and 42 per cent of men and women in 1984.[54] Although it is difficult to compare data from different surveys, because of different samples and different questions being asked, we know that even when both parents are working and earning a high salary the mother is expected to arrange for child care.[89] When a child is sick, the mother stays at home more frequently than the father (in 70 per cent of cases as reported by women and 50 per cent as reported by men).[112] There are, it seems, considerable differences and inconsistencies between what men and women report, women seeing the male contribution as being smaller than seen by men. When specific questions are asked about aspects of child care presumed to be the mother's responsibility, such as nappy changing, even wider discrepancies are seen between what mothers and fathers actually do. In one survey it transpired that 75 per cent of fathers had never changed a nappy, or only did so under protest.[82] Most fathers are happy to take their children out and play with them, their enthusiasm for doing so increasing with the child's age. Mothers change nappies, feed and bath, and perform all the tasks which bring them into the closest possible contact with their children. Fathers may love their children as much as mothers, but they touch less.

Mothers are more prepared to give up paid work as well as their career prospects.[71] Just under half of the population believe that 'a husband's role is to earn money; a wife's job is to look after the home and the family'.[112] One is tempted to add that in practice the majority believe that a mother's job is to earn money as well as to look after the home and the family. Maureen Green concludes in *Goodbye Father* that women today have too many roles, men too few.[44] This, of course, is not doing justice to the small number of fathers who are not only present in the labour ward, but also participate fully in all the exciting as well as mundane aspects of loving and caring for children.

All the men who are the subject of this book have a strong conviction that there is a very special bond between mother and child. A variety of explanations were offered, such as nature's intentions, the closeness of pregnancy, maternal instinct, the mother's dependence on her baby, the baby's preference for the mother and the opportunities that women have to learn about mothering. For some men the nature of the tie remains transcendental and mysterious, something which cannot be explained or verbalised.

Most men expressed the belief that fathers love their children as much as mothers do, and there is nothing that they cannot learn about baby/child care if they are willing; selfishness, lack of time and clumsiness were seen as the most formidable obstacles. It was thought to be beyond doubt that fathers do and should make an important contribution to the child's upbringing, but many men emphasised the difference between what mothers and fathers can offer. The child's age and sex were identified as significant factors.

The fathers in the study described various degrees of participation in the lives of their own children, and how they and their wives cooperated with each other. A few expressed the wish that the relationship could have been closer and some offered advice via myself to fathers generally.

Only a small number of men seemed to be totally convinced that gender plays no part in the quality of parenting, and a few have put these beliefs into practice. Most of the men who are bringing up their children alone, or had fully participated in their care, expressed a lingering doubt whether they had done it as well as a woman would.

Who should stay at home to look after a child, who enjoys being at home better and alternative child care arrangements were thought to be important issues. A few men felt that some mothers are excluding fathers, and that the law now favours women when a marriage breaks up by giving them custody.

The influence of culture and upbringing was found to play a part, but not always in the way that it might be assumed. Some men from very traditional cultures have internalised the values of their families of origin; most discarded them completely. Similarly, men who described a distant relationship with their own father do not necessarily wish to re-create this with their children. Many men expressed contradictory views on child care, saying both that gender does not and should not influence the quality of caring, and that women can do all sorts of things better than men.

The themes which emerge most strongly from these men's personal accounts are the deeply rooted belief in the uniqueness of the mother–child tie, division of tasks according to gender, full-hearted participation by some fathers and much ambivalence and confusion which many men are struggling with in relation to parenting.

Among the men who referred to how nature intends parents to behave is Alf (89, retired commercial traveller, widowed): 'It is in the woman's nature to fetch up children. They [women] are more patient, more loving, closer to the child.' Alf also referred to individual differences, 'there are some good and some bad mothers'. His own wife was 'a good mother' and was devoted to their daughter, but Alf also enjoyed the child's company. 'We went out for walks and went swimming.' Ralph (50s, teacher, divorced), who does not have any children, expressed his beliefs thus:

> There is a deep rapport between mother and child. Mothers do not look after children because it is their job. A child has an instinct to turn to its mother. I am not thinking about this from a moral point of view. It is just that in nature mothers and children are closer than fathers and children. Although there is lessening dependence on mother with age, my instinct is that mothers are better at looking after children whatever the child's age; there is the same design in nature for all creatures. Mothers understand the needs of the child, are more patient, more loving, better at ordinary nurture.

Ralph does not remember his own father, and was brought up in a totally female environment. Bert's summing up of how nature defines motherhood is in terms of feeding. 'Nature devised that women should feed children when they are born, the fathers cannot feed them. Nature also devised that mothers should look after them' (Bert, 87, retired fireman, widowed).

Pregnancy was often given as a reason for the special mother–child bond. 'Paternal instinct is much weaker than maternal, it is pregnancy which creates a special bond, particularly until the child goes to school' (Barry, 20, unemployed, single). Having said this Barry added that his sister has always been closer to his father, while he has been closer to his mother. Murray (23, student, cohabiting) is . . .

> Not quite sure, but if the woman has carried the child for nine months, there must be some special bond, whether a man could give it the same emotional feeding I have some doubts . . . but he could change nappies. . . . It is like having someone with you for nine months, you obviously have a good rapport with that person . . . it is mutual emotional feeding between mother and child and a man would find it difficult to break into this. I am not sure what happens when a child is adopted, if this [closeness to the child] is peculiar to mothers only or all women, but I don't think it is peculiar to men.

The belief that there is a maternal instinct was reflected in the following selection of comments, as well as in the ones already quoted: 'It is more instinctive for a woman to hold a baby, to cuddle and change nappies, it is more within their body' (Craig, 17, catering assistant, single); 'To feed and look after the baby is instinctive for the mother, even though a man would love it just as much' (Ramah, 19, unemployed, single).

A few men believe that mothers need their babies more than babies need their mothers. This view is strongly held by Keith (31, banker, single):

> It [the demand for closeness] comes from the woman and the child responds, because the child is too small to make a decision as to its own actions or to give a lot of vibes. Women form this dependence, a binding and a winding of things around them such as many spinsters do with cats. Men are much more independent, or think they are, the male attitude is probably more conditioning than nature. I am not sure if the female attitude is due to conditioning. Men are afraid that a small child may embarrass them, because it is so small and helpless. Women are so pleased to have something small dependent on them, that they themselves become dependent on it.

Keith referred to his father as an 'absentee father' and was mainly brought up by his mother in what he described as a Bohemian family.

A number of men believe that the baby, far from being passive and influenced by the parents, has a strong preference for the mother. 'Some women do not feel this closeness, but it is extremely important for the child, the child wants and needs it and the child should have the benefit of it' (Roland, 54, personnel officer, divorced). Karmi (47, lecturer, divorced) who was highly involved in bringing up his daughters, believes that 'the baby should be allowed to express his/her own preference and have some choice in which parent does what'.

Eamonn (59, social worker, divorced) has spent his life looking after others professionally as a nurse and social worker. For him the mother–child relationship is surrounded by a certain amount of mystique:

> From the beginning of time, women have been mother. The bonding that takes place is based on centuries of training, of giving birth. Men cannot have this tremendous interflow

between the mother and child, they can only watch it. Fathers can have tremendous love for the mother and the child but mothers have something special; this child has come out of her body. There is some special magic.

Whatever special endowment, predisposition and aptitude men ascribe to mothers, most of my informants thought that a man can learn to look after a child and that society is designed in such a way that the opportunity to acquire the necessary knowledge is less available to men than to women. For instance Vince (30, nurse, cohabiting) in the course of his nursing and midwifery career has made many relevant observations:

> There are still many men who are squeamish, or do not think it is their place or prefer to be down at the pub during birth. The mother spends more time with the baby after birth. If fathers were involved right from the beginning, they would be better at looking after babies. Antenatal classes are for mums. There is usually one token session for fathers. It is not pushed, it is not assumed that fathers will take on this role (looking after babies). Hospitals offer a session for fathers because they think they ought to, not because they want to. Fathers who are present at birth are mainly middle class. While the mother lies exhausted the father says more about the baby, but their interest is short-lived and the baby becomes the mother's responsibility. If the baby is not breast-fed both parents have the same responsibility and ability to learn how to look after it.

Jimmy (28, unemployed, single) also stressed that 'a mother would be better at feeding the child and buying its clothes, because she has had a chance to learn from her own mother but a man could learn; e.g. he could watch a film'. Simon (27, unemployed, single), who had a baby with his girlfriend, said that she was better at looking after her, having had experience as a child minder. If he has another child whose mother is inexperienced, he will be better at looking after the baby, having had some practice. Sanjay (32, taxi drive, married) believes that the bond between father and child 'can be created, once the child is born. He [father] can be present at birth. Physical care creates a bond.'

Many fathers who did not look after their children to the same extent as the mother, and also men who are not fathers, explained some of the reasons for the greater distances and being less expert at child care.

> Women are better at looking after children. Men would not be as gentle to begin with, but could learn. Men are afraid to handle a young baby, find it hard to judge their strength. In reality, a man is no more likely to hurt the child than a woman. Very few men would want to do for a child what a woman does. Men are more selfish (Lionel, 53, draughtsman, single).

Jacob's prescription is 'It should be the woman's job to look after the children. When the father comes home, he has done a hard day's work and he should be able to sit down and read the paper' (Jacob, 78, retired butcher, widowed).

A father's contribution was assigned great importance by everyone, even though it might differ from the mother's. Trevor (61, retired bank manager, married), who has three grown-up daughters, encourages participation:

> Mothers may be better at looking after children at all stages of their development but fathers should not be too eager to get on in the business world while the children are young. They should wait to climb the ladder of success until the children are older and do not need them so much as when they are young, otherwise the opportunity for closeness is lost.

Some men emphasised strongly that mothers and fathers are not interchangeable. One of them is Murray (previously quoted), who sees fathers as disciplinarians.

> A father can bring obvious coercive threats when the child throws a temper tantrum or when the child is older, say over 14. A woman is not physically equipped to deal with a violent child. My father could have taken away our pocket money.

Other special things that fathers can do were described in terms of play, taking the child out, treats, education and sports. According to Ivor (65, retired clerk, divorced), who has two daughters;

The father helps. Bringing up of children is joint, but changing nappies is different, it is the mother's job. Father should not take on the role of a dragon, some mothers create this role. A woman bringing up a boy cannot do certain things when he gets older, e.g. take him to football; a father who takes out his daughter swimming cannot go into the women's changing rooms.

There was no concensus of opinion on whether fathers are closer to their sons or daughters. However, most men felt that fathers have more in common with their sons, particularly as the boy gets older, in terms of special interests and activities. 'Men have a strong role to play, especially as the child gets older, as boys get more sporty and girls more grown up' (Keith, previously quoted). Craig (previously quoted) thinks that 'a dad can look after a boy better than after a girl, take him to football. Maybe it is not right but that is the way it goes . . . if boys and girls were brought up the same there would be nothing in life, it would be boring.'

It was thought that the age of the child is an important factor. Whereas some men thought a mother is better at looking after a child whatever the age, others thought that the older the child, the less s/he needed to be dependent on the mother and the father could share the caring more equally.

The men who are fathers themselves described their participation in child care ranging from occasionally playing with their children to bringing them up single-handed. Many men had done, and are still doing, 'special' things. When his children were young, Trevor (previously quoted) used to come home every lunchtime and his older two daughters used to fall asleep on his lap. By the time the youngest was born he had been moved to another branch of the bank, too far to bicycle home. He changed nappies and did everything his wife did, but not to the same extent, as she did not go out to work. Daniel (37, vicar, married) thinks that his wife is better 'at doing routine things and has more patience'. He looks after his children occasionally, e.g. takes them out, puts them to bed most nights and gives them a bath once a week, but 'could not see myself doing it all the time'.

A few men wish that while their children were young they had spent more time with them. Among these is Eamonn (previously quoted). His daughter was mostly looked after by his wife and maternal grandmother. Coming from a traditional Irish background he felt that this was how things should be, and the arrangements suited him at the time. Now he wishes that he had been closer to his daughter and had done more things with her.

Some men who do not yet have children said that they fully intend to participate in every aspect of child care, including feeding the baby – unless breast-fed – and changing nappies. Some fathers have put into practice their egalitarian principles. John (30s, photographer, married), whose wife also works, is very close to both his children, a boy aged two and a girl a few months old. He has done everything including nappy changing and bathing 'because it seems such an obvious way to be close to one's children'. He has, at times, noted some surprised reaction from his friends. Gerald (36, social worker, married) and his wife fostered a teenage boy: 'Our roles were totally interchangeable.' Karmi (previously quoted) spent more time looking after his daughters than did his ex-wife, as she was busy studying when they were young. One of his children became so attached to him that he 'could not take a photograph of her because every time I tried, she ran towards me'.

Two of the men are bringing up their children as single fathers. One of them believes that he has done it as well as the mother could have done. The other comes from a traditional culture in which men can be polygamous – his father had three wives and child care is a 'woman's job'. He has taken great pleasure in looking after his daughter, now 13 years old, ever since she was a baby, and as a single father who has her custody. He takes pride in her achievements and spends a great deal of time helping with school work and education in a much wider sense. In spite of this, he has a lingering doubt and wonders if a woman could have done some things better.

A few men expressed the fear of being pushed out by the mother when they become fathers; for example Leroy (23, unemployed, single) voices this anxiety:

> I would like to take a role in bringing up my kid. I wonder if a woman would get too possessive and keep me out. I would like to show him a lot of things and then let him fly, find out things and then come back. These days parents should share. Some men leave because there is not room to put their love and knowledge into the kid. There should be a part of the child's mind open to its father and a part open to its mother and the two parts should stay together. If we

split up, I would like to bring up the child. Fathers who get custody of their children are the lucky ones.

Chris (29, banker, single) also felt that 'justice is not always done when fathers are deprived of custody'.

Opinions were split on whether mothers should go out to work. There were those who believe that women not only should stay at home, but also like doing so, whereas a man would be very unhappy. Others said they themselves would be quite happy to stay at home and should be given the choice. Although some men would not want to be a full-time parent they thought their wives should have the same right and choice. 'If my wife wanted to go out to work I would be only too happy for her to do so', said Chris. However, he strongly believes that the parents should bring up their child the way they want to, and a child-minder could be a good or a bad influence. This concern was shared by others.

The question of which parent should stay at home if both wanted to go out to work was posed by me as a hypothetical one. Many men felt that it would depend on the circumstances, e.g. whoever earns less should give up paid work. On balance, most men thought that the mother should give up employment, either because she earns less, is better equipped to look after the child or it might be in the child's interest. There were, however, those who thought assumptions were unfair and that women are often forced into giving in. 'A woman may adopt the maternal role because of social pressures; there is no such thing as instinct' (Hugh, 37, lecturer, single).

Some men proposed a variety of solutions to sharing child care, such as both parents working part-time. The extended family and relatives helping out were also seen as beneficial, and relieving parents of sole responsibility.

Some men from very traditional backgrounds, such as Karmi, born in Iraq, met with disapproval from their own parents because of their high degree of participation in child care. Costas, born in Cyprus, did not think he would have been as involved in bringing up his children in his own country as he was in England. All the others coming from more traditional cultures are also a great deal closer to their children than were their fathers, in terms of physical care. Only 19-year-old Ramah intends to bring up his own children in a traditional way when he returns to Pakistan.

Many men seemed to be very unsure whether there is such a thing as instinct, whether women are better at looking after children and if parental roles are or should be totally interchangeable, and readily admitted their confusion; for example Ranjeev (26, nurse, cohabiting).

> It is the quality, not quantity, of parenting that is important. It is the couple's child and there is no difference. The initial attachment is between the mother and child, if the child is breast-fed, but this should not exclude the father. Fathers are often present at confinement. Their individual reactions are different but they do not go through the pain like the mother does. There is no 'natural instinct'. Both parents can understand the child. I will love my child and would give my life for it. I am not sure if there is a difference and if there is, what it is.

Troy (58, retired scientist, divorced) a father himself, reminisced:

> My wife was much more loving and caring, she wanted a child before I did. She took the decision. I spent a lot of time looking after our child. We shared the responsibility. My wife was not really better at it.

While the higher earning potential of men plays an important role in their lack of participation in child care it seems that some men lack confidence in their ability to be fully participant fathers. Most explain away their reluctance in terms of a mistaken – in my view – belief that mothers can offer something that fathers cannot.

9
Changing Attitudes

The term 'attitude' has been described in a variety of ways, but basically all of them suggest that it is a way in which a person's beliefs, feelings and behaviour are organised in relation to a psychologically significant concept or person. Its characteristics are that it has some continuity over time and is fairly resistant to change.[16] Attitudes to sex and gender issues have recently been explored by large-scale surveys,[54,55,71] which asked specific questions about legislation, equal opportunities in education and at work, housework, decision-making and child care. The most recent large-scale survey comes to the conclusion that

> While there was a widespread disapproval of formal obstacles to women's equality and of overt discrimination, there was much less evidence of attitude change in respect of the domestic division of labour which is a major cause of labour market inequality . . . an intriguing question remains . . . is the greater participation in the labour market by women likely to presage a change on the domestic front? Or does the process work the other way round?[112]

Comments about attitudes revealed that, with very few exceptions, the attitudes of the study men to gender issues have changed; some quite radically, others only to a minimal extent. Some men now hold egalitarian views, others still traditional ones and most are somewhere on the continuum between the extremes. By 'traditional' in this context is meant attitudes which support discrimination on the basis of gender, and 'egalitarian' those which essentially support total lack of discrimination apart from acknowledging biological differences. The men described the process of change as well as some significant ways in which the change had been achieved, such as through leaving school, making new friends, further education, cohabitation and marriage, also meeting women at work. Many men were not quite sure what had brought about change and a variety of factors, including inner motivation, were mentioned. Some men saw themselves as being swept along by something that was happening, e.g. the Women's Movement, and referred to the fact that 'society is changing'. Some men felt that it is easy to pay lip-service to egalitarianism while basic attitudes remain unchanged.

A few men, including the five eldest, did not think that their attitudes had or should change. They compared the younger generation unfavourably with their own, though they see better educational opportunities for boys and girls as an improvement. Their views are not without ambivalence. It is wrong – they said – to treat women as slaves, chain them to the kitchen sink. Yet they feel that greater freedom has resulted in weaker family ties, more divorces and delinquency.

Suggestions were made about how attitudes should and could be changed, and these included legislation and education. It was thought that women need to be more aggressive and less ambivalent about their stance. Many men, sympathetic to the idea of equality and supportive to the Women's Movement, expressed disapproval and fear of what they consider to be radical feminism and hostility of women to all men. A few see men as being disadvantaged, and consider that women are moving at a faster pace than men, and men need help to change. Change was described as a slow process which takes time to be accepted.

Most men did not think that women have achieved equality in education, and particularly at work. The concept of 'equality' was interpreted in many different ways and those who hold traditional views said that men and women are different and that, so far, any change has been a change for the worse. What seems to be characteristic of the attitude of many men of all ages, from different walks of life, is a great deal of confusion and uncertainty.

This is how the men whose views have changed describe the process:

> When I was 16 and came home from school, if my ironing was not done, I would have a go at my Mum. Now I am older, I realise what has to be done and it does not matter

who does it, a man can do it as well as a woman. (Craig, 17, catering assistant, single).

For Barry (20, unemployed, single) 'the change came from within and meeting girls'. Barry had been educated at a single-sex school and for him, like for many others of his age, meeting girls 'opened up a whole new world'. Richard (19, unemployed, single), also educated alongside other boys, said:

> It took me a long time to clarify things. It took a few years to get over the brainwashing I got at school, a hell of a lot of it. My mother and father did not mean to do it. I always felt there was something inside me that did not agree with a lot of things. I now go through my life trying to learn; through meeting people, talking.

Many men changed their views, having come from very traditional backgrounds, mainly during the process of higher education, through meeting others with egalitarian views. Among them were Nigel (Chapter 10: Individual Biographies) and John (30s, photographer, married) 'At university you were surrounded by people who were progressive in terms of their attitudes and thinking. My views are changing all the time, which is fortunate, because it is not happening all at once and you don't have to go crazy.'

Marriage has helped some men to change their views, e.g. Sanjay (32, taxi driver, married):

> At home it was drummed into us that a man goes out to work, a woman stays at home. It is not fair to expect the wife to do all the housework if both are working. Men miss out if they do not join in. If both do things together it becomes a pleasure, not so much a chore. Marriage changed my views. If I were on my own, I would probably still think that a woman's place is at home.

His wife works part-time.

Cohabitation was also quoted as a reason for change. 'Living with somebody makes you realise that you have to give and take. Living on your own you are egocentric', said Simon (27, unemployed, single). Hugh (37, lecturer, single) lived for several years with a woman who is a feminist. His views are highly egalitarian and to some extent have always been. 'A few years ago I would have given similar answers but I would have believed them less. I became educated through living with a feminist but could not have been sexist to live with her to begin with.'

Having children has helped some fathers to change, as has been the case with Harold (56, lecturer, divorced), whose views have never been conventional but are even less so now. 'I explored my capacity to relate to children and the way my children have responded to me.'

Working alongside women has influenced Donald's views. Donald (74, actor, divorced) has always had a lot of sympathy for women. 'I was not chauvinistic in my 20s. Working together in the theatre you often forget who is male, who is female. I have often helped women change if a quick change of costume was necessary.' Chris, who works in the City, has also worked with many women. He recognises that there are not many women on Boards of Directors, but has found that women are as intelligent and capable as men. 'A few years ago my views were nineteenth-century but now they are quite different' (Chris, 29, banker, single).

Some men remember their parents' segregated roles and the unhappiness it caused. They resolved to have a different approach to their relationships with women. Some consider such segregation very wrong on ideological grounds, e.g. Nigel (Chapter 10: Individual Biographies). A few men had parents or at least a mother who had egalitarian views. Bob (65, probation officer, single) described his mother as a feminist who was involved with the suffragettes and hated housework. 'I was never a chauvinist but my views have changed further in the direction of equality.'

Many men could not pinpoint any particular influence: 'things have changed' was given as the reason for personal change.

> When I was a young lad things were different. In the last ten years things have changed, it is a fact of life. I am a great pragmatist. If something is there, you accept it and play the game according to the rules. Society has brought about change, there have been changes through the ages. This change has come through enlightenment of men and women (Troy, 58, retired scientist).

Karmi (47, lecturer, divorced) enumerated many different influences:

> Contemplation . . . my early background, my profession, what I read, what I see, watch on TV . . . scientific works . . . deductive logic . . . past experience. You conform to a pattern and then establish your own stance.

Some older men believe that the younger generation have egalitarian views, whereas 'those over 40 have only nominally changed, as I have done' (Lionel, 55, draughtsman, single). Others also warn against paying lip-service only. 'Many men pretend that they treat women as an equal but really want to keep them in the kitchen' (Karmi, previously quoted).

Many suggestions were made about how attitudes can be changed. 'Passages from the Bible and the Koran should be removed. Page 3 of the *Sun* makes girls feel they are sex objects. There should be a law against people peddling such things' (Murray, 23, student, single). 'There is a big power struggle but we need more struggle to get rid of things like wars, violence and inequality' (Dick, 19, unemployed, single). According to Vince (30, nurse, cohabiting) 'there should be hard-sell publicity. It needs something that hits you between the eyes and makes you think. People do not take any notice of the softly, softly approach.' Roland (54, personnel officer, divorced) stressed the necessity for communication.

> Women should be prepared to talk to men in all kinds of situations: at home, in the work place, above all in the classroom. Social issues are grossly overlooked in the educational process. Men will lose out on their symbols of power. Once they recognise the lack of necessity for these, then I think there is a lot of satisfaction and joy to discover. It is there, it is just that you need to realise that social and human aspects are more important than material aspects of life.

The responsibility for changing attitudes was placed by some men on the shoulders of women. 'If you give a man a soft option he will take it' (Murray, previously quoted). He went on to express the view, also put forward by other men, that women have not availed themselves of the opportunities available:

> The opportunities are there, but women have not realised them, by not going into top jobs, not pursuing careers, not going into politics, getting married and tying themselves

down with children, not finding ways of coping with that
. . . my friend's wife, her attitude to equality is a non-starter
and many other women feel the same. If a man tells the
woman what she should do and she does it, he will say
'great', but if she refuses, he will have no choice. One of the
biggest hurdles to equality is women's attitudes.

Alan (21, unemployed, single) spoke about lack of opportunities in the field of employment. 'The hierarchy is made up so much of men that they don't let women in, women have to be more assertive.'

Some men felt that at times women want to have it 'both ways'. Karmi, for instance, thinks that women should not use their femininity to get promotion at work. 'They should be assertive, not use clothes and provocative make-up.' Vince (previously quoted) during his nursing career met some female fellow nurses who expected him to do certain things because of being a man.

In nursing, if a heavy patient needed to be lifted some
women used to call me because I am supposed to have the
muscle, but I am not as strong as some women. If there was
an intruder in the hospital grounds, it was me who was
always sent out and I was more frightened than some of the
female nurses.

Strong views were expressed by some men, who see themselves as highly egalitarian, about what they see as radical feminism. 'Women who want to become earth mothers, get rid of all men, are out of touch. If equality is going to mean something, it has to embrace everybody, not just certain groups you consider you are equal with' (Murray, previously quoted). Sanjay (previously quoted) is opposed to extremism in all forms.

I don't believe in women's lib and I do not believe in
chauvinism. I believe men and women can get along fine, if
only they met halfway. Let men do the jobs women do and
women the jobs men do – it would be a happier world. If
God wanted us to be the same, he would have made one sex.

Daniel (37, vicar, married) distinguishes between what he considers feminism and extreme feminism:

There are all shades of feminism. If it is about drawing attention to inequalities, to men and women having equal opportunities, I have the greatest sympathy, I favour it very much. The more extreme forms I find disturbing but I recognise that inequality gives rise to anger. It is not right to say that lesbian relationships are more valid and authentic than heterosexual ones. A woman should not be excluded from a commune because she has a male baby.

Two men have been personally very deeply hurt by some feminists and still have highly egalitarian views 'in spite of this'. Both of them have also been hurt by prejudice, one because of his colour, the other because of being gay. Ranjeev (26, nurse, cohabiting) described how in a professional discussion he was 'shocked and hurt quite badly. They [some colleagues] pushed me into a corner and I had to defend myself. I am not a child abuser or potential rapist.' Vince (previously quoted), who is gay, also described occasions when, in spite of being very sympathetic and supportive to the Women's Movement, he felt attacked and intimidated by women who seemed to hate him simply because he is a man.

Men like Roland (previously quoted) feel that older men particularly:

> have lost out in this change very badly. They have the tendency to be less adept socially, less able to express feelings. Women have a slightly biased attitude. They should be fair to men and help them change.

Change was described as a slow process. Karmi (previously quoted) believes that 'change can only take place slowly through education, not legislation'. Troy (previously quoted) also thinks that time is needed for any change to be effective. 'Any change takes at least 30 years and we have only been talking about this sort of thing (attitudes to sex and gender) for 10 years.' Harold (previously quoted) points out the discrepancy between the expectations of men and women.

> Women are trying to rush it. Men will come round to it. Women want to move quicker than men are prepared to agree. Anything like this, new law, new ides, at first there are objections. A lot of men are afraid of losing their jobs, of competition.

The question whether women have achieved equality was interpreted in a number of ways, depending mainly on the basic attitude to sex and gender issues. Those few men who openly voiced their belief that men and women should be treated differently because they are different thought that things should be left as they are. Any change that has and was likely to take place would not be an improvement. Many men recognised that there are some areas, such as employment, where women are still discriminated against, but did not think that men and women are or should be interchangeable within the family, especially in regard to bringing up children. A few both recognised the existence of inequalities and would like to see a radical change, but were fairly pessimistic about it and thought it would take a long time before a transition to a society in which there is no discrimination could be effected. With very few exceptions, equal opportunities legislation was supported, but some men doubted its effectiveness.

Many men spoke openly about feeling uncertain about their stance on gender issues. Others revealed their uncertainty by what appeared to be highly contradictory statements. Pronouncements about basic similarities between the sexes were qualified by descriptions of differences. Sanjay (previously quoted), having said that there is no difference other than biological, later added: 'let nature take its course, women are more gentle, more feeling, less aggressive. They are the pretty things of the world; in nature there are poodles and there are guard dogs.' Alex (54, scientist, divorced), having said that there is intellectual equality, countered this by ascribing to men the ability to be more analytical and inventive. Lionel (previously quoted) believes that there are basic differences but was surprised to find through attending a therapy group 'how similar men and women are'.

Those who 'believe' in equal educational opportunities for boys and girls made some remarkable exclusions. For instance, Trevor (61, retired bank manager, married) would draw a line at some subjects. 'I would not encourage a boy to knit, it would be considered cissified.' Jonathan (17, unemployed, single) having said that boys and girls at his school were treated in exactly the same way, related that 'at [his] school, boys got more shouted at but also got more encouraged'.

Equality at work as an ideal was often combined with reservations. Leroy (23, unemployed, single), while adopting equality, assumes that a woman would not cope well with an emergency and a man may have greater presence of mind and capacity for decisive action. Clifford (64, clerk, single), in spite of his egalitarian attitude said:

> If I were to go into a booking office and find a female booking clerk, I would feel that there was something distinctly odd. I cannot defend it, there is nothing logical about it. It is instinct. There is something within everybody that likes things well ordered. If something goes against it, you get a jolt. One may accept it with one's mind, but it makes you uneasy.

Those who share housework with their partners on an equal footing still tend to make one or two assumptions about allocation of tasks. Laundry, especially sorting out of clothes, is seen as something women do better, as in the case of Gerald (36, social worker, married). Other men who are or had been married openly admitted that, as was the case with Ralph (50s, teacher, divorced), strong moral egalitarian principles were not put into practice. Ivor (65, retired clerk, divorced), whose second wife went out to work, said 'She also did most of the housework. It should be equally divided. It did not start like this, but it developed [into unequal shares].'

Those who saw decision-making as ideally joint also sometimes felt like Jeremy (62, sculptor, divorced) that 'it should be a man's privilege in some instances'. He also expressed the opinion that women are mentally tougher; as capable, if not more, of resolving important issues.

Some men, like Stanley (23, money dealer, single) would be happy for their wife to work and contribute her income but would also like her to stay at home and would enjoy being able to support her. Some of those advocating a joint account were unhappy when their wives had equal control, and wanted to retain ultimate authority over money matters.

In the area of personal relationships most men said that they wanted women to behave in the same way as men, but many expressed surprise when a woman approached them first. Taking turns at paying on occasions when the couple go out was combined with the belief that the man should be responsible in certain circumstances, e.g. in a public place, and that paying the bill is a way of showing affection.

Child care is an area in which the greatest ambivalence was

expressed. Adam (21, unemployed, single), for instance, having said that both parents can care for a baby equally well, later on confided:

> I would like to be more like a woman with a baby, more gentle, sensitive, loving and caring. They [women] feel more, their feelings are nearer the surface, they are sort of proud that they have feelings.

Costas, who had been highly participant in the care of his children, admitted that he could easily have slipped into traditional ways and would have done it in Cyprus, where he was born. Donald (previously quoted), having said that it is the mother who should stay at home to look after the child if there is ultimate disagreement, also suggested that 'the deciding factor should be the respective earning capacity of both parents'. Bob (previously quoted) insisted both that mothers are better at caring for children and qualified this by remembering meeting a number of fathers through his work as a probation officer, who were claiming custody and 'seemed to be the more suitable parent to take on daily care'.

About equality, and whether it has been achieved, among others Lionel (already quoted) had this to say: 'Men and women have not achieved equality, but what more is there to achieve?'

Among the men who are very aware of their uncertainties is Daniel (previously quoted):

> Intellectually, I know there are very few differences. Within me, I feel there are. In an ideal world people should be free and valued for what they are. It should be acceptable for a man to stay at home and society should be so ordered that this can be accommodated. Within myself, because I am traditional, there are aspects of femininity that I value, such as being caring and maternal. Instinctively, I expect a woman to be gentle. I cannot imagine myself marrying a woman who was not. The issue of equality is particularly acute within my profession [the Church]. I find myself torn. The Church of England has excluded women from the priesthood. It is difficult to reconcile the position of the Church with equality. The Church has connived in a social order in which women are in subordinate positions. Women are excluded from power and responsibility. I believe in

equality and I have reverence for tradition. We have identified priesthood with authority, yet the Scriptures teach us that it is about service.

The doubts expressed in this statement are the main theme of Daniel's attitude as they are of Eamonn's (59, social worker, divorced):

I have this schizophrenic attitude to women. In a work situation I work alongside them and treat them as equals. In a close relationship I want them to be somebody else: gentle, loving, caring. I could go to work the next morning and the same woman could be my boss and I would accept the fact. At home, I want her to be feminine. I am asking an awful lot. It may be impossible. The home is something else, the work scene is something else. I expect a woman to play a number of roles but I also expect it of myself. Very Irish but then that is me.

Eamonn sums up the attitudes of many men in this book, wherever they come from, both young and old, across social classes. His statement and all the others quoted illustrate male confusion in the 1980s.

10
Individual Biographies

Emile Durkheim, the father of modern sociology, claimed that social facts such as norms and rules of behaviour exist in their own right, and that one set of such facts may cause another. For him the study of individuals was irrelevant to the understanding of social processes. Since then, the study of individuals and small groups has become sociologically respectable, each person being recognised as an actor whose performance is idiosyncratic in style, but who is also acted upon by the environment. In turn, that environment does not remain constant; it can be changed through the conscious effort of the actors.

The three men whose life histories, attitudes and actions will be fully described illustrate the way in which individual actors look to the past and the future, want to preserve the *status quo* as well as being motivated by a desire for change. Tom, Graham and Nigel have been chosen to illustrate these tensions and contradictions, because they are in many respects very different from each other. They come from different backgrounds, follow different occupations, and represent a wide age range. All three are subjected to similar pressures exerted by the process of social change. While Nigel wants to change the world, Tom's reaction is more in the nature of 'Stop the world, I want to get off'. Graham would like to travel in both directions, into the future and into the past, because the present does not appear too comfortable. All three have been very frank and honest in their disclosures but may have elected to do so for different reasons. Tom and Nigel made it clear that they had a strong point of view on how the world should be arranged – though their conceptions of a proper social order are diametrically opposed. Graham, I suspect, was quite glad to share his feeling of uncertainty and his experience of

Individual Biographies

conflict of values and of contradiction between some of his norms and how he actually lives his life in his suburban environment.

When I first met Tom, born and bred in the East End of London, he was putting away his paintbrushes having just finished a day's work on a conservatory of a large Victorian house. With some pride he pointed out that it had been much in need of renovating and he was pleased, as was the owner of the house, with the result. At the age of 78, Tom remains very active and continues to work part-time at his lifelong occupation of painter and decorator, having been self-employed since his retirement. He was intrigued at the idea of a woman writing a book about men, particularly because, so far, he had not credited the women he had known with much ability to concentrate. 'When you try to talk to a woman, you find that after the first few minutes she has stopped listening.' He hastily modified this frankly expressed opinion by adding that some women were different and credited me with possibly being one such anomaly. Having agreed to talk to me he also invited me to talk to his wife, who would confirm that they have been happily married for 57 years. When I politely declined, Tom seemed pleased to learn that it was his own views which were being sought.

At first, we spoke about Tom's past life. His father, like himself, was in the building trade and his mother stayed at home to look after a large family. Tom left school at 14 and took the first job that was offered, 'selling goods from the back of a lorry'. Looking back, he regrets not having the opportunities which children have nowadays to continue their education beyond the earliest school-leaving age. Apart from the war years, when he worked in the gas works, Tom has been a painter and decorator since the age of 15. He met his wife when still very young and married her when he was 21. He recalled buying her an engagement ring and sought my views on whether I could envisage this ever being the other way round. He found the idea of a girl buying her boyfriend a ring extremely amusing. The first child, a girl, was born after Tom and Mary had been married for five years, Mary having given up her job while she was pregnant. Two boys followed at well-spaced-out five-yearly intervals – all children being very much wanted and no preference being given to the boys. Tom frankly expressed strong disapproval of mothers going out to work outside the home.

In them days the first thing a child would ask when he or she came home from school was 'where is my mum?' Today it is different and more likely to be 'what's on the telly?' . . . Nowadays, mum is at work and the kiddy has got the key . . . mum used to have her finger on the pulse, she knew what was happening.

Tom disapproves of mothers who use child-minders to look after their children, 'it is not right to take a little kiddy on a bus at seven o'clock in the morning'. Also, when both parents go out to work the child can become unruly and all they have time for is to admonish the child in the evening rather than monitor the child's behaviour during the day. According to Tom, women are discontented as a result of doing two jobs: paid work and housework at the same time. The women who can afford nannies have more freedom of choice to go out to work or sit on committees – even though 'a nanny is not a proper mum' but a good enough substitute. In Tom's view the bond between a mother and her child is totally different from that between father and child, 'there is a different understanding'. A father, however, can love his children as much as a mother, while being closer to a boy, the mother being better able to understand the needs of a baby girl. Tom is convinced that the child's sex makes a substantial difference and remembers loving his own children equally, but differently. Parental feelings are influenced by 'looking forward to the future . . . a father would be looking forward to playing games with his son'. Tom recalled playing roughly with his boys, but 'it was only natural that the girl wanted to play with dolls'. From about the age of three, Tom remembers a definite difference in the way he played with his own children and how they themselves wanted to play.

Tom 'knows' that a man could not look after a child of any age as well as a woman, because women have more patience. He gave an example of a child refusing to get up in the morning. A mother would cajole the child and 'keep on', whereas a man would 'only say it once and then lose his patience'. Tom's children are now middle-aged and have all been married. Alas, his daughter got divorced and never remarried. Tom feels sad about this. One of the sons and his wife have had twins. Their mother is a Cordon Bleu cook and while the children were young taught at evening classes, so that she could always be at home with the children when her husband was at work – an arrangement which Tom, as grandfather, strongly approved of in accordance with his conviction that a woman should put her family first on the list of priorities.

On the subject of education, Tom has mixed views. He welcomes better opportunities for both boys and girls, and wishes that they had existed in his time. He is strongly aware that achievement is still related to money and social class, middle-class children having a better chance of succeeding than working-class ones. In his days it was unheard of that a working-class child would learn to speak French. He considers such subjects as languages to be suitable for both boys and girls. There are also subjects, such as metalwork and needlecraft, which should not be equally available to both sexes as 'it is more natural for a girl to learn to sew and for a boy to learn carpentry'. He justified this by explaining that there has always been some unemployment, and at a time when it is particularly high it would not be fair for women to compete for the same jobs as men. Tom does not share Mrs Thatcher's belief that the national cake can get bigger, and that there will be enough work for all. He sees men and women as competitors in the field of employment. He believes that there are some jobs that a woman could never do, because of inferior physical strength. Women are best at teaching or being secretaries, and can be good doctors. Tom disapproves of men and women mixing too freely at work 'because they are different and it is not right for a woman to wear trousers and a man to wear earrings'. With regards to equal pay Tom's views are egalitarian: it should be the rate for the job, otherwise lower rates for women would eventually affect men also as the rate for the job would become lower for everyone.

Tom sees the male role mainly as providing material resources for his family, as did his own father.

> It is a man's place to provide . . . it would be unnatural for a man to stay at home. In the society I was born in it was the accepted thing, once you left school, to look for a job . . . you took whatever job was going, you could not be fussy.

Tom puts a strong emphasis on money and class determinants of one's lifestyle. He considers that those with a college education have more choices and do not have to concentrate on just earning a living to the same extent as a working-class man. Also, there is money left for other things over and above providing for the family. 'It is only natural that there are different levels of society.'

The idea that there is some kind of natural order which determines relationships between social classes as well as men and women runs as a strong undercurrent in all Tom's beliefs.

He considers men and women to be very different creatures by nature, in terms of intellect, emotions, social and personal relationships, expectations and aspirations. The most fundamental difference between the sexes in Tom's experience is that women lack a sense of humour. They cannot tell or laugh at a joke; therefore, Tom prefers to have a good laugh with his male friends. Women are easily impressed and more easily influenced than men, which makes women easy prey to advertising. A woman would be more likely to buy a newly advertised product than a man.

> Women are deceived by appearances, man looks under the surface . . . for men, basics come first . . . a man works for necessities, a woman works for extras. To appear to do the right thing a woman would go a long way to a wedding or a funeral.

Regarding friendship, Tom considers that both sexes need friends, but meet their friends and spend their time together in different ways. Again, he emphasises class distinctions. A working-class woman with young children may not have much time to spend with friends; a middle-class woman can entertain at home. A man is more likely to meet other men at work, who would be regarded as colleagues rather than friends. Male and female expectations and behaviour within intimate relationships are also seen by Tom as different. During courtship it is again 'natural' for the man to take the initiative, pay for entertainment and buy the ring. Once the couple are married, Tom believes that a woman's whole life revolves round her relationship with her husband and children, which determines the depth of her feelings towards them. A man, while at wok, has other interests. Tom was not sure if unemployment, compelling men to stay at home, would make a difference, since he generally believes that a woman's feelings are basically different: a woman is more loving, more patient and less aggressive than a man.

Tom subscribes to a double moral standard in personal relationships:

> If a man has an affair it does not matter, because it is not

going to take him away from his wife, and she will still be there . . . a man is not likely to give his affections outside marriage and, therefore, provided he looks after his family financially, an affair is not likely to break up a marriage. A woman goes head over heels if she has an affair and this could lead to a divorce.

The main cause of men having affairs is diagnosed by Tom as the difference between men and women in their sexual appetite after the age of 45:

> After 40 or 45 a woman has lost all interest in sex and looks upon her man as a meal ticket, a man goes on being interested in sex – just like Charlie Chaplin. . . . A woman is as old as she looks, a man is old when he stops looking.

Tom believes that women should make themselves attractive and disapproves of jeans and unisex fashions. Likewise, he objects to men wearing jewellery. He would not have been attracted to a woman who was '50 per cent a man'.

He believes in strict division of domestic labour: cleaning and cooking are 'women's work'. At the same time he disapproves of men who cannot look after themselves if necessary: 'a man should be able to look after himself if he has to, not rely on Chinese takeaways'. A widowed man, or even one retired, is at a disadvantage, compared with a woman, who can follow her usual occupation of being a housewife. A man is used to being looked after, 'having his meals cooked for him and his socks mended' – as Tom's wife has always done for him.

On the subject of finance, Tom's views and practice have been very egalitarian. He has always considered the money he has earned as belonging to himself and his wife jointly, and they have made together all major decisions regarding spending. Tom has never had a bank account and there not being much left over after paying for basics has meant little financial manoeuvrability. Tom considers it morally wrong for a man to conceal from his wife what he earns, or not to share his income, though in cases where the wife is 'a big spender' the husband might have to curb her expenditure and exercise some control.

Tom's views have not changed over the years, and he has put into practice what he believes. He is one of the few men whose attitudes and beliefs have at all times coincided with his actions, and he has few regrets. He has lived a happy life but would have liked a better education and more money. He talks with nostalgia about how things used to be, and sees today's society as too materialistic, this being the cause of many people's dissatisfaction and family breakup.

> Women have lost out. They have gone for the shadow and lost the substance . . . they have lost a happy home life. People expect too much these days.

Overall, Tom sees women as different creatures from men, and believes in strict division of labour both within the house and in the workplace. Even when his views are egalitarian, such as on the subject of equal pay, his position is meant to benefit men, rather than women. His convictions are firmly held and genuine, and have their own congruence and consistency. He is aware that the world has changed, but as far as he is concerned this is not for the better.

Graham, at the age of 45, has recently taken on more responsibility at work, having been offered and accepted promotion to headmaster of a school. The setting for our talk was a large Victorian house in a London suburb, with the rear window overlooking a leafy, secluded garden where Graham, his wife and two young children can jointly escape into semi-rural tranquillity during those precious moments when Graham is neither working at school nor planning a new timetable while taking a bath or a shower. One is very aware that Graham is under a great deal of pressure at work. His wife, Mary, is a full-time housewife, without whose back-up her husband could not cope with his paid work. Graham began to talk to me in a somewhat apologetic vein as, prior to our encounter, he had not thought about male/female issues deeply enough, although they often enter into after-dinner conversations. In his daily life he is surrounded by more women than men: his wife, daughter, a mother who lives nearby and female colleagues, who at his school outnumber men by ten to one.

Graham's early days were fairly middle-class and materially comfortable. His father was a salesman and his mother a civil servant, who went out to work as well as taking the main responsibility for the children and housework. Graham was educated at a local primary school, followed by a grammar school and teachers' training college. Careerwise his advancement has been steady, from a primary school teacher, to deputy head, to headmaster. He has been married ten years and has two children.

On the subject of similarities and differences between men and women, Graham's views are very mixed. Intellectually be believes there is no difference, while being very aware that subtle discrimination exists at all levels: curriculum, different rewards for different subjects and behaviour and social expectations which in turn affect performance. In terms of aptitudes, Graham believes that there is a difference: women tending to excel in some fields such as verbal ability. Girls, in his experience, begin to talk sooner than boys and more quickly acquire an extensive vocabulary. This capacity, according to Graham, is innate and in turn leads to women being more emotionally responsive than men.

> When I have a problem I would not dream of talking it over with a male friend, I prefer to talk to a woman friend. It is not that boys and girls feel differently, or that men and women do, it is just that they express themselves differently. Women are ten times more empathic than men.

Graham continued by sharing his surprise at his own frequent inability to pick up subtle clues during social encounters.

> I am constantly amazed at my own lack of understanding of other people's emotions. When my wife and I meet another couple, afterwards she might say 'Have you noticed such and such?' For instance, the other woman might have looked upset or anxious and I am cursing myself for not noticing such an obvious fact. It [empathy] is a game which women have been playing for decades.

Graham indicated that awareness of how others feel is something a man could learn with practice but, so far, not many men have practised, with the exception of certain professionals such as therapists, psychiatrists and clairvoyants.

Boys and girls, according to Graham, have very different interests from an early age. He has noticed this difference from about the age of three in his own children but, on reflection, recalled buying sex-typed toys. 'The first toy I bought for my daughter was a hoover, you cannot be more sexist.' The boy tends to be interested in cars; not surprisingly so, since his mother does not drive and the family car is always driven by Dad, whether on family outings or with Graham at the driving wheel taking off for work and reappearing at the end of the day. The boy's original car game was to arrange them into geometrical lines – as though they were a substitute for bricks. Only as he grew older did he begin to use them as little replicas of the real thing. It was when they started going to a nursery that they began to make definitive pronouncements about boys' and girls' toys, and on the basis of such segregation made judgements such as 'boys don't play with this', with regards to dolls and vacuum cleaners.

Moving into education, his specialist field, Graham believes that:

> Entitlement to education should be uncluttered by teachers' prejudices and expectations. Boys and girls will equally excel at the same subjects. Boys and girls should be able to learn together, as well as to have some time with their own sex; for instance, girls should have time on their own, away from boys, who try to dominate them and show their superiority.

A recent survey has shown that mixed education does not necessarily benefit girls, because of the tendency that boys have to show off and put girls down.[29] Graham is concerned not only about open discrimination, but also about the hidden agenda, teachers discriminating against girls in a variety of subtle ways such as praising them more for appearance, neatness and good behaviour than for academic achievement.

In the field of paid work, men and women can do similar jobs – except where male muscular strength and female empathy and patience are required. However, one essential advantage which men have is the ease with which they command respect.

> Lurking at the back of my mind is the father as number one idea in Christianity. I cannot help feeling that a man in authority has this quality of being a father figure, like in a family, people would be more likely to trust him, to trust his judgement. It is a feeling I have but I know it is wrong to feel like this. When some members of my staff relate to me, they are seeking a reliable, trustworthy father figure who will listen to them and not let them down.

Individual Biographies

It is worth commenting that Graham was brought up by his grandfather, a strong and reliable man, in comparison with whom his mother was a much weaker though loving, person. Graham's own father left the family when Graham was one year old. Another advantage which men have is, paradoxically, a result of a disadvantage, said Graham:

> Because of their weakness on the emotional side, men are better at distancing themselves and making a rational decision . . . I would not be saying what I am saying except in these circumstances [for the purpose of the interview] because, politically, I am against what I am saying . . . in some ways it goes against the grain . . . I am very mixed up.

Rationally, Graham believes that there should be equal opportunities for males and females of all ages, both in education and employment as well as equal pay. Emotionally he does not.

Moving into the area of personal relationships. Graham again expressed egalitarian views, while emphasising some differences. He has not himself had any male friends since leaving school and has a definite preference for female company and friendships. He regrets and fears the possibility that such platonic friendships might be misinterpreted by his wife and others, because of the sexual connotations involved in social stereotypes of male/female relations, and which can be false and restrict choice.

Close male/female relationships, again, are an area of confusion in terms of beliefs, values and standards. 'Women are more dependent on men than men on women, but it sounds like real nonsense as soon as I have said it.' He explained that what he meant was that women invest more in relationships and, therefore, investment rather than dependence are key variables. Both sexes can be equally loving, but men are more capable of detaching themselves from love and seeing things rationally. Women have a more romantic expectation from marriage than men – even little girls play at weddings and look forward to a white dress and being happy ever after. Men are more action-oriented – concerned with what they will do, rather than how they will feel. When a marriage goes wrong, Graham believes that it should be terminated through separation or divorce. He does not approve of open marriages and does not subscribe to a double moral standard; for as long as the marriage is happy, neither partner should look outside the relationship for sexual satisfaction.

According to Graham, major decisions can be made jointly, and if they cannot be reached they should be shelved for a time. In case of major disagreements which could not be resolved, and had to be settled urgently, his wife would have the last word on anything that concerns the children, such as their health and schooling, while Graham would make the final decisions about finance and moving to another area. He firmly believes that money, whoever earns it, belongs to the family, and that the partner who is not in paid employment should have the same decision-making rights as the wage-earner. He feels embarrassed when his wife consults him before buying clothes for herself, as action such implies how she feels as the partner doing unpaid work at home. Graham considers that a working man and his non-working wife, and the other way round, are joint partners in business, running it together and jointly entitled to the profits.

When I put to Graham the question about housework, he laughed, with some unease, and told me that this was a difficult area, specially for some men who bring work home – not necessarily their briefcases full of files but 'work' could include just thinking creatively, generating new ideas or organising an office system from one's bathtub filled with hot water. There are considerable differences between various jobs and the demands they make. A motor mechanic can, at the end of the day, wash his hands and face and be free from work until the next day. Many professional men, and Graham is one of them, would not be able to cope with their job without being serviced by another person. Before he got married Graham had a cleaning lady. Since marriage his wife has to a large extent looked after his domestic needs. He acknowledges that it is only fair that they should both do the housework. Graham is not quite sure how the arrangement about paid work and staying at home were arrived at between his wife and himself, it just seemed natural that she should give up her job to look after the first baby, and then the other child followed and the question of her returning to full-time work has never arisen. On the subject of child care, Graham has fairly inflexible views.

> My gut reaction is that a woman is both better at it and has a stronger moral obligation to perform a myriad of daily chores. Mothers have special qualities which make them better at child care . . . they are more forgiving than men . . . when they get cross and angry with the child they are

> more capable of switching off quickly and redirecting the child by saying 'let's do something else instead'. Men find this hard. Women have more foresight in thinking of the children's needs and their state of tiredness. They are not necessarily better than men at organising activities such as play . . . what I really feel is that the best solution would be job sharing.

Graham comes home tired after a long working day; sometimes he stays behind quite late to see the parents of his pupils, or to attend meetings. When he gets home at night there is little time and energy just to be with and do things with his family. His well-intended promises to cook an evening meal once a week have not materialised. At times his wife is also very tired, having done a full day's work at home, and Graham feels that he is not doing his 50 per cent of housework. This way both Graham and his wife are not totally satisfied, whereas a job share would give them both an interest outside the home and more chance to be with their children.

> People should be able to apply for jobs, making it clear that they have a family and choose the number of days which they want to work. There are bound to be people who want to work four days a week and others only one day, which would create a perfect fit.

Graham's attitudes have changed over the years, and used to be much more traditional. Fifteen years ago he 'would have laughed at some of my questions'. This change has been brought about by awareness of social change, meeting and talking with people interested in the male/female issues.

> As a result of the equal opportunity debate – and I support equality – a great strain has been placed on men. I have a demanding job and come home tired but then I feel guilty that I am not doing my share of the housework. The feminist movement has done a lot of good for women . . . I am not so sure what good it has done for men.

While listening to Graham, I was reminded of some of the characters in Phillip Hodson's book *Men*[47] whose lives are dominated by work and who find it hard to get off the treadmill.

Nigel, a graphic designer in his early 30s, has been politically active as a member of his trade union and the Labour Party. His views are radical and based on a keen awareness of the social forces which mould individual biographies. His early working-class upbringing was highly conventional. His father was a manual worker and his mother a nurse, who combined paid work with another full-time job of mother and housewife. Nigel's only sister continues the family tradition by having opted for a conventional marriage, motherhood and full-time domesticity. According to his parents, Nigel's lifestyle and views are very unconventional: 'I am something that they read about in the Sunday papers' – not their idea of a son. Nigel's education has been state throughout, and after leaving school he continued to study and obtained a degree in art.

He has never been married, but has had a number of heterosexual relationships, the current one being with a married woman who is estranged from her husband. While at university, Nigel met Donna, with whom he lived for ten years; the relationship has only recently come to and end. They have remained on good terms and the friendship includes Donna's current partner.

Nigel thinks that there are very few differences between men and women, and believes in absolute equality. Such differences as do exist are mainly due to social conditioning, but some to biology, and there are some physical experiences such as menstruation, pregnancy and childbirth which women go through and which, lying outside the scope of male physical experience, have to remain something that males and females cannot fully share.

> Men do not experience childbirth, women do. Because of this there are differences which relate to pain and body structure. Women are better at bearing pain, men make a fuss. Men cannot feel the same kind of pain as women do.

From his own experience of being close to a number of women, Nigel has learned something about pain and discomfort which can be felt during menstruation. Although able to show concern and ask what he could do to help as well as 'make cups of tea', he felt inadequate, and aware that his empathy was based on guesswork rather than true identification. Unlike men, women also experience the emotional pain caused by unwanted pregnancy or fear of such if they do not use contraceptives or find them unreliable. Donna had two abortions while he was living with her. There have been occasions when Nigel was told by his female friends that he could not fully understand what they were feeling, and he could only agree with this. It has been said in his book *Men* by Phillip Hodson,[47] a counsellor who has spoken with many men about problems related to their relationships with women, that men are afraid of female sexuality. Melanie Klein, a psychoanalyst, described and analysed some of the terrifying fantasies which men have of being harmed by women, as well as envy of the mother's ability to bear children and her capacity to feed and nourish them. Nigel's reaction to female sexuality seems to be a desire for a fuller understanding, as well as an awareness that some aspects of it will remain an eternal mystery for the male.

> Most gender differences that exist are caused by conditioning and male oppression of women. A woman can say to me 'You don't know what it is like to be a working-class woman, having to stay at home and look after young children.'

Nigel believes that working-class women have a particularly bad deal, fewer choices and are more likely to be depressed as a result of having to give up paid work and having to stay at home to look after young children. According to the findings of a major survey,[17] this is very true, and there is a difference in the incidence of depression between middle-class and working-class women, being much higher among the latter.

Physically Nigel is slightly built and does not consider himself to be particularly strong. Although some men – not himself – possess superior physical strength, he does not consider this to be particularly advantageous for the performance of strenuous tasks, since there are not many of these left and in future, due to modern technology, there will be even fewer. In the last analysis there are some tasks which do require physical strength, but not as many as is generally assumed.

Most of Nigel's friends are now women and non-sexist men. He has not had a close male friend since his school days and the nature of his friendships has changed considerably since he entered higher education. Until then, friendships 'revolved around sex and drinking' and certain subjects were unmentionable. For instance, feelings were a taboo subject among men, and women were talked about as sexual objects. Between working-class males this was done in a more obvious way than between middle-class ones. Nigel prefers close friendships with women rather than men, because women are more open about their feelings and have more empathy with others – both due to social conditioning. Ideally, both men and women should make the same kind of investment in a friendship and are, Nigel believes, capable of this. Many relationships break down because of external factors – things that are not generated within the relationship itself. As an example of this, Nigel referred to fidelity between the sexes in a close relationship. Ideally, he believes that all relationships should be open, and that sexual fidelity imposes a very narrow definition on the nature of close personal relationships. It is wrong to single out sex and to regard it as different from intellectual companionship or non-sexual love. People do not usually mind sharing their friends with others when this involves intellectual and other interests and pursuits; therefore the criterion of exclusivity, when applied to sex alone, makes an artificial and false distinction between sexual and other types of feelings and activities. Such distinction is due to social norms and imposed values to which Nigel 'reluctantly and irrationally' has himself subscribed. Sexual 'betrayal' is the only kind that he cannot tolerate and accept neither in himself nor his partners. Finding out about unfaithfulness has always felt as a personal hurt and, when committed by himself, as a guilt-generating secret, since he believes that all relationships should be based on honesty and equality, and that eventually a more advanced society will encompass open sexual relationships which will replace those based on possessiveness and jealousy. Unfaithfulness, as we understand it now, will become a meaningless concept, and convention will be replaced by individually negotiated agreements. However, in present-day society, dominated by the ideal of monogamy, those who rebel against this norm cannot escape feelings of guilt and discomfort generated both from outside and inside oneself. Whenever Nigel has had to resort to 'abusing the other person's trust' by having affairs outside the main relationship he has himself condemned his inability to be open about this. His longstanding relationship eventually came to an end because, among other reasons, he learned that his partner had also had other relationships, and Nigel was unable to tolerate this.

The penalties for violating a social norm are heavy, and although there are many standards of behaviour and many norms, monogamy still appears to be favoured by the majority of the population.[54] While, intellectually, Nigel is well able to argue the case for a polygamous structure, emotionally he has been conditioned to reject it. 'Most people, including myself, have a lot of hangups, regarding sex. What is really important is that people should respect rather than make use of each other.' He recently declined an offer by a woman who wanted to have a time-limited three-month relationship while her living-in boyfriend was away for that length of time. This would have meant that the relationship could not have developed naturally and Nigel would have been used to fill the gap and meet somebody else's need, with total disregard for his own. He does not believe that sexual behaviour should be related to gender. He has at times initiated relationships by taking the first step, without regarding himself as a male chauvinist, because he genuinely believes that women also should feel quite free to approach a man to whom they are sexually attracted. The notion of female passivity, and the wish to be hunted, is a myth.

How money is used both in transient and stable relationships can be an indication of who has the power, and the principle to which Nigel is most attracted is that whoever has most money contributes most, but when the couple are living together, all money is considered as joint. After the necessities have been paid for, the balance should be divided equally, and each party retain control of their share – as an insurance against the 'big spender disposing of all the money'. Nigel has been out with women better off than himself, who paid the bill, and also in reverse situations – both arrangements feeling equally right and comfortable.

When two people live together, whether married or not, housework is not the exclusive responsibility of either sex. What in Nigel's view is important, is the time available, and this depends on the work which the partners do outside the house. 'Whoever gets home first should cook or get done whatever needs to be done ... expecting the woman to do all the housework is one aspect of male exploitation.'

Nigel's views on child care are well thought out and based on his political ideology and personal encounters with couples who have children, as well as on the arrangements in his family of origin and that of his sister's. He voiced strong disapproval of women giving up paid work to look after children, unless they are genuinely happy and wanting to choose between working at home and paid employment in favour of the former. He would expect the mother of his own child to return to work, after finding a child-minder, and himself to participate fully in bringing up his child. He has seen many women who had decided to stay at home becoming unhappy and losing an interest in themselves and everything else.

> What happens is that there is a radical change when a woman has a child. . . . I think that children have a role, but that role is not to dominate . . . . I have observed what has happened with my sister and her children . . . the children dominate everything . . . all the discussions. Women spend a number of years bringing up children and when the youngest is 18, what do the parents have left? They have nothing left . . . I have seen it with my own parents.

There is undeniably a great deal of enjoyment to be had from bringing up children. Nigel is very aware of this, and that sacrifices are also necessary, but considers many such sacrifices beneficial neither to the children or the parents. How much has to be sacrificed depends on social class and conditions of employment. 'In our society a working-class woman may have very little to sacrifice – except a boring, monotonous job.' Hers is, therefore, a Hobson's choice. Here again, material conditions determine personal choices as they do in other areas.

Nigel's attitudes have changed since leaving school and his early environment, mainly through educational opportunities and meeting a different set of people. The woman with whom he lived has also been an important influence on his way of thinking. On reflection, Nigel added that if his beliefs and ideas had been all that conservative, and traditionally opposed to the feminist perspective, he would not have chosen to live with an outspoken feminist, and if he had, the relationship would not have survived and flourished for as long as it did. Most people are seen by Nigel as being bound and constrained by their social environment, their class affiliation and membership, and having limited opportunities for changing their beliefs, widening their understanding and altering their attitudes or patterns of behaviour. He considers himself lucky in this respect. His own parents still behave as they did when they were first married, and play their traditional roles in spite of them both being at home, having retired, and Nigel's mother having had a major operation which has left her less physically strong than before. Nigel believes that they could have lived much fuller lives, and been much happier, had they been able to get out of the groove and relate to each other on a more equal basis. He is also concerned for his sister, who has elected to be a full-time mother and housewife and sees a boring and unpromising future in front of her; the world will have changed and when the children are grown up she will have very little in common and hardly anything to talk about with people who will have kept in touch with things. 'She may become a boring person, and in spite of what she has sacrificed for her family they may not even appreciate it.' Nigel does not subscribe to the view expressed by Penelope Leach[58] that mothering, as a full-time occupation, should be granted a more elevated status. His parent's views on many issues are radically different from Nigel's. They disapproved of his liaison with Donna, and feel that now he 'has nothing to show for it'. Presumably 'something to show' would have been a wife, a semi-detached house and children. Nigel, himself, feels that he has taken away a great deal from the relationship, in terms of understanding and ideas about male/female closeness and intimacy. He has decided not to tell his parents about the current relationship, since they would be bound to view it with much conventional disapproval. 'My mother is 63 and my father is 81 – there is no point in arguing with them and putting them into an early grave by upsetting them.' Certain subjects are therefore avoided and taboo when Nigel goes to visit his parents. He often feels like cooking the Sunday lunch for the family, but knows that this would only upset his mother, as she considers cooking as both her duty and her prerogative. Nigel feels a certain amount of discomfort caused by the awareness that he treats the women in his family (his mother and sister) differently from the way he treats all other women. He does not argue or openly talk about his views with his mother, particularly for fear of upsetting her without affecting any change.

Change in human relationships has to come about as a result of a more fundamental social change.

> You cannot abolish sexism, until you abolish capitalism. No matter how aware I am as an individual, I still opress women because of being a man in this society. Consciously, I do not set out to opress women, but maybe there are other things I can do, such as being more active in my trade union. I am conscious of inequalities, but how much do I do to combat them?

Individual Biographies

It is men like Nigel, who are most likely to contribute to change by direct action, involvement in pressure groups, membership of political organisations and putting his principles into practice. Graham, one suspects, might well be happier in an environment in which he was subjected to fewer pressures. Many men in prestigious occupations with a career structure which includes promotion are subjected to the greatest amount of pressure simultaneously at work and within their families.[113] A job share would free him from an ongoing conflict. There is little doubt that Tom has no incentive to promote equality between the sexes. He has been prepared to suffer female 'lack of humour and inability to hold an intelligent conversation' in exchange for the home comforts which have been provided by 'the Mrs', and being looked after has been ample compensation for female shortcomings.

References

1. Ambrose, P., Harper, J. and Pemberton, R. (1983) *Surviving divorce – men beyond marriage*. Wheatsheaf Books, Brighton
2. Argyle, M. and Henderson, M. (1985) *The anatomy of relationships*, Heinemann, London
3. Aries, P. (1973) *Centuries of childhood*, Penguin, Harmondsworth (originally published 1962)
4. Bateson, G. (1973) *Steps to an ecology of mind*, Paladin, London
5. Bee, H. (1974) *Social issues in developmental psychology*, Harper & Row, London
6. Bee, H. (1981) *The developing child*, Harper & Row, London
7. Bee, H. and Mitchell, S. (1984) *The developing person*, Harper & Row, London
8. Bem, S.L. (1974) The measurement of psychological androgyny, *Journal of Consulting and Clinical Psychology*, 42 155-62
9. Bowlby, J. (1951) *Maternal care and mental health*, HMSO, London
10. Bowlby, J. (1953) *Child care and the growth of love*, Penguin, Harmondsworth
11. Bowlby, J. (1958) The nature of the child's tie to his mother, *International Journal of Psychoanalysis*, 39, 350-73
12. Bowlby, J. (1969) *Attachment and loss*, vol 1: *Attachment*, Hogarth Press, London
13. Bowlby, J. (1973) *Attachment and loss*, vol 2: *Separation: anxiety and anger*, Hogarth Press, London
14. Bowlby, J. (1980) *Attachment and loss*, vol 3: *Loss*, Hogarth Press, London
15. Broverman, I.K., Vogel, S.R., Broverman D., Clarkson, F.E. and Rozenkranz, P.S. (1972) Sex role stereotypes: a current appraisal, *Journal of Social Issues*, 28, 59-79
16. Brown, R. and Herrnstein, R. (1975) *Psychology*, Methuen, London
17. Brown, G. and Harris, Tirril (1979) *Social origins of depression*, Tavistock Publications, London
18. Burlingham, D. and Freud, A. (1944) *Infants without families*, Allen & Unwin, London
19. Central Health Service Council (1959) *The welfare of children in hospital*, Report of the Committee, HMSO, London (the Platt Report)
20. Central Statistical Office (1985) *Social trends*, vol. 15, HMSO, London
21. Central Statistical Office (1986) *Social trends*, vol. 16, HMSO, London
22. Chester, R. and Peel, J. (eds) (1977) *Equalities and inequalities in family life*, Academic Press, London
23. Chodorow, N. (1978) *The reproduction of mothering: psychoanalysis and the sociology of gender*, University of California Press, Berkeley
24. Coleman, D.A. (1977) *Assortative mating in Britain*. In R. Chester and J. Peel, (eds), *Equalities and inequalities in family life*, Academic Press, London

References

25. Corbin, M. (ed.) (1978) *The couple*, Penguin, Harmondsworth
26. Dominian, J. (1968) *Marital breakdown*, Penguin, Harmondsworth
27. Eekelar, J. and Clive, E. with Clarke, R. and Raikes, S. (1977) *Custody after divorce*, SSRC Centre for Socio-Legal Studies, Oxford
28. Equal Opportunities Commission (1983) *An equal start*, EOC, Manchester
29. Equal Opportunities Commission (1984) *Girls and information technology*, EOC, Manchester
29a. Equal Opportunities Commission (1985) *Do you provide equal educational opportunities?*, EOC, Manchester.
30. Equal Opportunities Commission (1986) *10th Annual Report and Women and Men in Britain*, HMSO, London
31. Firestone, S. (1971) *The dialectic of sex, the case for a feminist revolution*, Jonathan Cape, London
32. Flandrin, J.L. (1979) *Families in former times*, Cambridge University Press, Cambridge
33. Fletcher, R. (1975) *Marriage and the family in Britain*, revised edn, Penguin, Harmondsworth
34. Franks, H. (1984) *Goodbye Tarzan*, Allen & Unwin, London
35. Freud, S. (1925) *Some psychological consequences of the anatomical distinction between the sexes*. In *The Works of Sigmund Freud*, vol. V, Hogarth Press, London (1950)
36. Freud, S. and Breuer, J. (1883–85) *Studies on hysteria*. In *Collected Works*, vol. II, Hogarth Press, London (1955)
37. Friedan, B. (1977) *It changed my life: writings on the Women's Movement*, Norton, London (1985 edn)
38. Fromm, E. (1957) *The art of loving*, Allen & Unwin, 1971, London (originally published 1957)
39. George, V. and Wilding, P. (1972) *Motherless Families*, Routledge & Kegan Paul, London
40. Goldberg, S. (1977) *The inevitability of patriarchy*, Maurice Temple Smith, London
41. Goode, W.J. (1956) *After divorce*, Free Press, Glencoe, Illinois
42. Gorer, G. (1955) *Exploring English character*, Cresset Press, London
43. Gorer, G. (1971) *Sex and marriage in England today*, Nelson, London
44. Green, M. (1976) *Goodbye father*, Routledge & Kegan Paul, London
45. Hart, N. (1976) *When marriage ends*, Tavistock Publications, London
46. Headlam Wells, J. and Holt, A. (1986) *Opting for different worlds*, Humberside College of Further Education, Professional Centre Publications, Hull
47. Hodson, P. (1984) *Men*, Ariel Books, BBC, London
48. Homans, G. (1961) *Social behaviour: its elementary forms*, Routledge & Kegan Paul, London
49. Home Office (1974) *Equality for women*,. Cmnd 5724, HMSO, London
50. Home Office (1979) *Marriage matters*, a consultative document by the Working Party on Marriage Guidance, HMSO, London
51. *The I Ching* (1951) translated by R. Wilhelm, Routledge & Kegan Paul, London
52. Irvine, J., Miles, I. and Evans, J. (eds) (1979) *Demystifying social statistics*, Pluto Press, London

References

53. Jacobs, A. (1986) Married to an invalid, *The Sunday Times*. 27 April
54. Jowell, R. and Airey, C. (eds) (1984) *British social attitudes*, Gower, Aldershot
55. Jowell, R. and Witherspoon, S. (eds) (1985) *British social attitudes*, Gower, Aldershot
56. Kidd, T. (1982) Social security and the family. In J. Reid and E. Wormald (eds) *Sex differences in Britain*, Grant McIntyre, London
57. Laing, R. and Esterson, A. (1964) *Sanity, madness and the family*, Tavistock, London
58. Leach, P. (1979) *Who cares? A new deal for mothers and their small children*, Penguin, Harmondsworth
59. Leonard Barker, D. and Allen, S. (1976) *Dependence and exploitation in work and marriage*, Longman, London
60. Letts, P. (1983) *Double struggle*, National Council for One-Parent Families, London
61. Lidz, T. (1977) *The family and human adaptation*, International University Press, USA (originally published 1963)
62. Littlewood, B. (1978) South Italian Couples. In M. Corbin (ed) *The couple*, Penguin, Harmondsworth
63. Maccoby, E. and Jacklin, C. (1974) *The psychology of sex differences*, Stamford University Press, Stamford, California
64. McKee, L. and O'Brien, M. (eds) (1982) *The father figure*, Tavistock, London
65. Mahoney, P. (1986) *Schools for the boys*, Hutchinson, London
66. Maidment, S. (1981) *Child custody: what chance for fathers?*, National Council for One-Parent Families, London
67. Maidment, S. (1984) *Child custody and divorce*, Croom Helm, London
68. Malinowski, B. (1929) *The sexual life of savages in North Western Malanesia*, Routledge, London
69. Marsh, C. (1982) *The survey method: the contribution of surveys to sociological explanation*, Allen & Unwin, London
70. Marsden, D. (1969) *Mothers alone*, Allen Lane, London
71. Martin, J. and Roberts, C. (1984) *Women and employment*, HMSO, London
72. Mead, M. (1963) *Sex and temperament in three primitive societies*, Morrow, New York
73. Millett, K. (1971) *Sexual politics*, Rupert Hart Davis, London
74. Mitchell, A. (1981) *Someone to turn to*, Aberdeen University Press, Aberdeen
75. Mitchell, A. (1985) *Children in the middle*, Tavistock, London
76. Morgan, D. (1985) *The family, politics and social theory*, Routledge & Kegan Paul, London
77. National Council for One-Parent Families (1987) *Annual Report*, NCOPF, London
78. Newson, J. and Newson, E. (1965) *Patterns of infant care in an urban community*, Pelican, London
79. Newson, J. and Newson, E. (1968) *Four year old in an urban community*, Pelican, London
80. Newson, J. and Newson, E. (1976) *Seven year old in the home environment*, Pelican, London

References

81. Nicholson, J. (1984) *Men and women*, Oxford University Press, Oxford
82. Oakley, A. (1974) *The sociology of housework*, Martin Robertson, Oxford
83. Oakley, A. and Oakley, R. (1979) Sexism in official statistics. In J. Irvine, I. Miles and J. Evans (eds) *Demystifying social statistics*, Pluto Press, London
84. Oakley, A. (1981) *From here to maternity*, Penguin, Harmondsworth (first published as *Becoming mother*, Martin Robertson, 1979, Oxford)
85. Office of Population Censuses and Surveys (1980) *Classification of Occupations*, HMSO, London
86. Office of Population Censuses and Surveys (1981) Census, 1981, Preliminary Report, HMSO, London
87. Parke, R.D. (1981) *Fathering*, Fontana, London
88. Parsons, T. and Bales, R. (1956) *Family, socialisation and interaction process*, Routledge & Kegan Paul, London
89. Rapoport, R. and Rapoport, R.N. (1976) *Dual career families re-examined*, 2nd edn, Martin Robertson, Oxford
90. Reid, I. and Wormald, E. (eds) (1982) *Sex differences in Britain*, Grant McIntyre, London
91. Richards, M. (1980) *Infancy*, Harper & Row, London
92. Richards, M. (1982) Post-divorce arrangements for children: a psychological perspective, *Journal of Social Welfare Law*, May, pp. 133–51
93. Richards, M. (1982) How should we approach the study of fathers? In L. McKee and M O'Brien (eds) *The father figure*, Tavistock, London
94. Rimmer, L. and Popay, J. (1982) The family at work, *Employment Gazette*, June
95. Robertson, J. (1962) *Hospitals and children: a parent's-eye view*, Gollancz, London
96. Rowlands, P. (1980) *Saturday parent*, Allen & Unwin, London
97. Rutter, M. (1972) *Maternal deprivation re-assessed*, Penguin, Harmondsworth
98. Schaffer, R. (1977) *Mothering*, Fontana, London
99. Shorter, E. (1976) *The making of the modern family*, Collins, London
100. Skynner, R.A.C. (1976) *One flesh, separate persons*, Constable, London
101. Stone, L. (1979) *The family, sex and marriage in England, 1500–1800*, Weidenfeld & Nicholson, London
102. Storr, A. (ed) (1983) *Jung: selected writings*, Fontana, London
103. Tavris, C. and Offir, C. (1977) *The longest war: sex differences in perspective*, Harcourt Brace Jovanovich, New York
104. Thornes, B. and Collard, J. (1979) *Who divorces*, Routledge & Kegan Paul, London
105. Townsend, P. (1979) *Poverty in the United Kingdom*, Penguin, Harmondsworth
106. Walczak, Y. with Burns, S. (1984) *Divorce: the child's point of view*, Harper & Row, London
107. Wallerstein, J. and Kelly, J.B. (1980) *Surviving the breakup – how children and parents cope with divorce*, Grant McIntyre, London

References

108. Weiss, R. (1975) *Marital separation*, Basic Books, New York
109. Wilson, E. (1977) *Women in the welfare state*, Tavistock, London
110. Wing, R.L. (1979) *The I Ching Chinese workbook*, Aquarian Press, Wellingborough
111. Winnicott, D.W. (1958) *Collected papers*, Tavistock, London
112. Witherspoon, S. (1985) *Sex roles and gender issues*. In R. Jowell and S. Witherspoon (eds) *British social attitudes*, Gower, Aldershot
113. Young, M. and Willmott, P. (1973) *The symmetrical family*, Routledge & Kegan Paul, London

Index

Acts of Parliament see statutes
affective individualism 114
age of informants 8
androgyny 2, 31
anima 28
animus 28
anthropoligical perspective 18
aptitudes 50-2
attitudes 129-39
   and cohabitation 131
   and marriage 93
   change of 2, 129-39
   of informants 130-9
   see also British Social Attitudes

biographies of individual informants 140-58
bonding 2, 122, 123
British Social Attitudes 1, 11, 18, 106

Census (1981) 1, 64
   (1851) 63
characteristics male/female 1, 27, 29-31
   desirable 31
   neutral 31
   undesirable 29, 30
   see also differences, and differences and similarities, stereotypes
child care 4, 59, 99, 127
children 114-28
   and fathers 34, 114-28 *passim*
   and mortality rates 115
   and mothers 34, 37, 114-28 *passim*
   and parental behaviour 34
   and psychoanalysis 116
   historical perspective 114
   views of informants of parenting 120-8
cognitive theory 35
cohabitation 11, 78, 131
conception 32
confusion about differences and similarities 128, 136, 139
courtship 83-8
   and money 86-8
   historical perspective 83, 84
   who initiates 83-6
couvade 30
Croydon Local Education Authority 56

decisions 105-8
   about residence 106
   and earnings of spouses 105
   rules and metarules in 106
   to divorce 106
   views of informants on who should make 107-8
demographic changes 8, 9
development, child 32-8
   emotional 34
   physical 32-3
   prenatal 32
   psychosexual 27, 28 117
   pubertal 33
differences male/female 23-56 *passim*
   beliefs unfounded 37
   between mothers and fathers 114-19
   established 37
   explanations of 30-2, 37
   historical perspective 26-9
   physical in adults 33-4
   physical in children 32-3
   see also differences and similarities
differences and similarities, views of informants 39-53
   aptitudes 50-3
   emotional 42-8
   intellectual 39-42
   interests 48-50
   see also characteristics male/female, courtship, development, employment, friendship, love, marriage, stereotypes
discrimination 3
   in education 60-1
   in employment 67, 77, 136
   psychological theories justifying 3
divorce 10, 80, 95, 96
   views of informants on 96, 97

Index

dramatis personae 5-7

education 53-63
  further 57
  higher 58
  of sample 5
  primary 56
  views of informants 58-63
  see also discrimination in education, GCE, subject options, teachers

employment 66-77
  part time 66
  pattern of male/female 65-6
  pre-industrialisation 65
  reasons for 68, 69
  segregation of men and women 67
  trends in male/female 9
  views of informants 69-77
Equal Opportunities Commission 55, 67
ethnic origin 14
  of sample 14
European Court of Human Justice 4

family
  and unequal power 106
  of origin of sample 15
feelings *see* emotional development, differences emotional, similarities and differences/emotional
feminism 134, 135, 136
  see also Women's Movement
friendship 78-83
  views of informants 78-83

gender 1, 26, 28, 79
  identity formation in children 35-6
General Certificate of Education (GCE) 57
  results 57
  subject choices 57

homogamy 89
homophobia 79
homosexual unions 88
housework 98-105
  and women's dissatisfaction 98
  statistics relating to 98
  views of informants on 99-105
hysteria 29

I Ching 27
instinct 51, 121, 127
interests 48-50
  maternal and paternal compared 121, 122

labour
  division of 2, 3, 99
  exclusion of women from statistics 64
  see also employment
Legal Aid 10
love 84
  father and mother 117, 119
  in marriage 89-98 *passim*

R. de Mannerville 116
marriage 88-97
  age at 10
  and employment 69
  and sex 90, 91
  breakup 95, 96
  expectations from 10, 89, 90
  motives for 89
menstruation 28, 152

occupations of sample 12
  see also Registrar General's classification of

patriarchy 31
pay
  average of men and women 4
  equal 64, 76, 77
  relative of husbands and wives 109
periods see menstruation
poverty 9
pregnancy 107, 121, 152
psychoanalytic theory 35
  see also development prenatal, decisions
puberty see development

questionnaire 18-24

Registrar General's classification of occupations and social class 8, 13, 19
relationships see cohabitation, courtship, friendship,

165

Index

homosexual unions, marriage religion 28

sample description 5–16
  see also dramatis personae, education, ethnic origin, family of origin, occupation (of sample)
  schools 55, 58
  leaving age 10
  see also education, teachers
sex
  biological 26, 36
  extramarital 93, 94
  see also development in childhood, puberty; gender, marriage and sex
sexism 1, 157
similarities male/female *see* differences and similarities
single parents 11, 66
  in sample 126
social class 13, 50
social learning theory 35
Social Security benefits 11
socialisation 36, 79
Statutes
  Education Act 1944 58
  Employment Protection Act 1975 69
  Guardianship Act 1973 11
  Guardianship of Infants Act 1925 116
  Legal Aid and Advice Act 1949 95
  Matrimonial Proceedings Act 1984 11
  National Assistance Act 1948 11
  Sex Discrimination Act 1975 4, 58
  Social Security Act 1973 11
Stereotypes 29, 30, 32, 35–8, 57
  in education 55, 57
  in employment 67, 68
  research on 36–8
Subject options at school 54, 56, 57
Survey method described 16–25
  see also questionnaire

teachers 55, 56
  see also education, subject options
toys 34, 54, 55
trade unions 9

unemployment 3, 15, 65, 105

Welfare State different treatment of men and women 63
witchcraft 28
Women into Science and Engineering (WISE) 56
Women's Movement 3, 47, 151
  and attitude change in men 130, 135
  and child care 115
work force
  proportion of men and women 65
  see also employment

Yin and Yang 26, 27